God's Miracles in My Life

By

Tillie Hogans

© 2003 by Tillie Hogans. All rights reserved.

No part of this book may be reproduced, stored in a retrieval system, or transmitted by any means, electronic, mechanical, photocopying, recording, or otherwise, without written permission from the author.

ISBN: 1-4107-5487-1 (e-book)
ISBN: 1-4107-5486-3 (Paperback)
ISBN: 1-4107-5485-5 (Dust Jacket)

This book is printed on acid free paper.

1stBooks - rev. 09/24/03

"A Psalm of David"

The Lord is my shepherd; I shall not want. He maketh me to lie down in green pastures; He restoreth my soul; he leadeth me in the paths of righteousness for his name's sake. Yea, though I walk through the valley of the shadow of death, I will fear no evil; for Thou art with me; thy rod and thy staff they comfort me. Thou preparest a table before me in the presence of mine enemies; Thou anointest my head with oil; my cup runneth over. Surely goodness and mercy shall follow me all the days of my life; and I will dwell in the house of the Lord forever.

(intro)

Advice I Give to the World

There is nothing impossible with God. I can tell the world that God is real and I recommend him to the reader of this book. With the use of one hand, I was able to achieve my goals and overcome my obstacles. God has walked with me and talked with me when I wanted to give up. He was carrying me when I didn't even know it. We are living in a cruel world now. I will let you know drugs are not the answer, dropping out of school and being a parent at an early age is not the answer. Put God first and He will enable you to be whatever you strive to be. You can be your own enemy. Don't let anyone tell you what you can't do. Make the first step and God will do the rest. There are so many people that are bound and trapped. I pray this story will break the barriers in their lives. Writing this book was hard for me. It took praying and asking God for guidance, wisdom, and patience to get through each part. I would start writing my book and then I would put it down for a period of time. The grace and mercy of God got me through. I am writing this book to the world, especially to people who are handicapped or cannot cope with life. I hope that the things I went through, fighting for my life as a baby, will be an inspiration to people and have an impact on their lives.

(the beginning)

Part I

This book is about me, a miracle child. My name is Tillie Lee Hogans. I was born March 16, 1953 in a little town in North Florida called Defuniak Springs. My parents are William and Ruth Hogans. I have four sisters and two brothers: Cheryll, Marsha, Gloria, Brenda, William and Obra, and a cousin Claudia. Osselena Goode was a special woman whom I will never forget; she was my favorite grandmother. She played an important role in my life. My mother once told me that at the age of two I was walking and in good health.

My father and mother decided to go for a ride. They stopped the car near a friend's house because they were having car problems. We visited mother's friend, Julia White, who had a precious baby boy named Troy, and I wanted to get down and play with the baby. Mother wouldn't let me, because the baby Troy was sick and had a fever. Julia didn't know what was wrong with him. She finally decided to let me get down and play with him. They didn't have vaccine shots in that town. While I was on the floor, I suddenly went into a terrible seizure. I was rushed to Pensacola Baptist Hospital, where I was placed on an "iron lung." I was a very sick child from then after. The doctors told my family I had polio and that I wasn't going to survive. I was paralyzed all over. Mother told me, I contracted a disease called polio and that my right arm would retract up constantly. The doctors had placed a sand bag to keep my right arm from retracting. My mother thought my nerves in my right arm were destroyed by the polio.

I could not use any of my limbs at all. I stayed in the hospital for three years, with a brace on my back and legs. I was fighting for my life. The therapy helped me recover the use of my left arm, and I began to learn how to walk again. I never recovered the use of my right arm, but the feelings are still there. I was a sick child, although I knew that it was the grace of God that kept me alive; I have so much to be thankful for. I acknowledge my family for staying by my side throughout my illness those three years. I knew it was hard for them to travel up and down the highway. During that time, my family didn't know if I was going to make it through.

Through all types of therapy on my legs, the doctors and nurses were successful in molding my limbs, all except for my right hand. I didn't have the use of my arm; all I had was my feeling without any movement at all. I had to wear special shoes because I have clubfeet and had a limp when I walked.

I stayed in the hospital so long that it seemed like it was my home. My family would always come to see me and check on me. After spending three long years in the hospital, the doctors finally released me, but I really didn't want to leave the family I had grown to know in the hospital. However, I had to go home.

The doctors told my mother after I had returned home that I could walk, but I was pretending that I couldn't, so they carried me around everywhere. However, one day they decided to fool me, I was sitting in a chair when they told me they were leaving to go somewhere and I was waiting for them to pick me up. Well, they wouldn't and they were headed out the door when I got up and walked. Then after, I was able to do the things other children did.

My Mother

This poem is about a very special person that has not been told;
I tell you her name is Ruth Hogans, her Christianity shows as she travels this road;
My mother raised me up in the church;
That's how I learned always put God first;
There were times when I got out of line;
Just the look on her face, I knew the next step was going to be a spanking on my behind;
My sickness, going to the doctors and my falling tears;
You could always depend on her; she was always near.
Through my strides, pains, and darkened nights,
My mother was at my rescue to make things right;
I know there were times I let the devil get the best of me,
But through God's chastisement He made me see;
I can't express with a thousand tongues all the things you have done;
For me all my childhood life;
She looked beyond my faults and saw the good inside;
Because of my mother I wanted to succeed and stop holding my pride back;
Thank You, Jesus for my mother that I love so much…
I love you mother, for God gave you to me and I am so touched…

(main body)

I can truly say I have so many *positive things* I can address. I will first address *reverence for GOD*, if it had not been for Him, I would have died at an early age, but he spared my life; because I feel He had a mission on earth for me and it wasn't my time to go. From an *early age* GOD was always in my life. I learned to master many *handicaps,* and obstacles that were in my way. First, I had to recognize that I had a disability and learn how to deal with it. You have to love yourself first; that's very important. We all have a handicap, whether it's physical, mental, or spiritual. The decision is based on you. The *steps* you take in life cost you your life.

There are many positive things in my life: my spiritual walk with GOD, having that inner peace knowing that GOD has never left me through any storm that faced me in life. To know the peace of GOD is to lack for nothing. There were times in my life when it was like a ship on a stormy sea. The trials can be very rough, and the struggle can be fearsome. There were times when I felt like I was losing control, but then I learned how to rise above the waters; the heavy seas cannot threaten me; the fact is GOD was carrying me every time, no matter how the storm may rage around me. I know that GOD is my refuge and my fortress, He is my light and my salvation. I do not have to fear but I would walk with Him, talk with Him and meditate. Believe me, it takes that in this lifetime. I have faith that I am a conquerer, not a failure, that GOD has a plan for me in my life.

Reverence for GOD, Who has always been in my life. I know for myself that He is real and there is nothing impossible, nothing that He can't do. I was the one who was chosen from my mother's womb to go through a difficult test as I walked with GOD. It wasn't easy as I faced trials and situations and having to deal with people.

I can say GOD is good; He is good all the time. I am the type of person that it didn't matter who you were, I love people in all shapes and colors. That's part of my character. I go out of my way helping people. But there have been times when some people took my kindness and it has cost me some hardship in my life for being the person I am. There is a saying that goes, "GOD gives you common sense." That is true, but sometimes it does not happen in that way; you live and you learn, and you have faith, and you pray that you do not continue to keep making the same mistakes over and over again. As I get closer to the LORD, I begin to ask him to direct my path, order my steps, teach me what to say and what not to say to anyone. It took a long time to get to this point. You see, I have been hurt so much and let down in my life. You get to the point in your life where you do not know who to trust anymore. When I try to do good evil will always present itself. When I take to God everything that perplexes my mind, nothing is to great for Him to bear, for He holds up the worlds, He rules over all the affairs of the universe. There is no chapter in our experience too dark for Him to read; There is no perplexity too difficult for Him to unravel. When I say that, I mean it from the depth of my soul. I know He lives inside of me and I am a born-again Christian. In all of my doubts, perplexities, temptation, hours of loneliness, JESUS was always there to help me overcome my disappointments, troubles, and sorrows, even when I felt like I could not go another step, and my back was against the wall. I had no one I felt like I wanted to confide in, but "JESUS" because I know if you tell JESUS something you do not have to worry about it. He will handle any situation in His time, but you have to wait on Him. Patience is the key of anyone's life, having the patience and faith to wait on GOD to work it out for you. What I mean by this statement is that He knows what's best for us. We think sometimes we want this, whatever it may be. But, GOD knows what lies ahead for us, and sometimes that what we think we want is not good for us. I thank GOD for that, because when I look back on my life and some of the things I have asked GOD for and I didn't get, believe me, I am so glad; if I had a chance to relive everything I did in the past I would not be caught up in what people said or thought about me. He always intervened for me to come out on top. This poem that I wrote has a big impact on me. No matter what you are going through, if you hang on in there, GOD will make it all right. Though at your darkest hour, before day, joy will come, and you will have that peace in JESUS name.

There is Peace in Jesus Name
When you are down and feeling depressed;
Do not have no one to turn to
Look up to JESUS, I tell you He is the Best!

There is always hope and peace in JESUS name;
Get in the spirit and let his anointed
Power flow through you
Try it you'll never be the same.

Satan is busy going to and fro;

To see whom he can deceive
If you're not careful, he will steal your joy
And have you where you don't believe.
JESUS cares when you're in sorrow and burden
And in so much pain that is so hard to bear;
I can recommend there is peace in JESUS name.
JESUS love and his word is the only thing can keep us;
Acknowledge him in all things; He is the only one You can trust.
So when you find yourself up against the wall;
Go down on your knees and pray. He will never Let you fall.

Reverences to GOD: there were times I would like to be alone, where I could meditate and hear from GOD. I would turn off my television for days and be shut up in my bedroom praying and seeking GOD. I could feel the presence of the Holy Spirit vibrating, putting His spirit on me. I began to cry out, and I started praising the LORD. You know no matter how bad things are or seem to be, you still have to praise GOD for the bad as well as for the good, even when you don't feel like it. I can promise you when you do that, it is when GOD intercedes on your behalf. I have always read my bible, everything I needed to know was in GOD's words. Whenever fear tried to come upon me, I would start saying Psalm 27:

Tillie Hogans

"A Psalm of David"

The Lord is my light and my salvation;
Whom shall I fear? The Lord is the strength of
My life; of whom shall I be afraid?
When the wicked, even mine enemies and my foes,
Came upon me to eat up my flesh, they
Stumbled and fell.
Though an host should encamp against me,
My heart shall not fear; though war should rise
Against me, in this will I be confident.
One thing have I desired of the Lord, that will
I seek after; that I may dwell in the house of the
Lord all the days of my life, to behold the beauty
Of the Lord, and to inquire in His temple.
For in the time of trouble He shall hide me in his pavilion:
In the secret of his tabernacle shall He hide me;
He shall set me up upon a rock.
And now shall mine head be lifted up above
Mine enemies round about me; therefore will I
Offer in His tabernacle sacrifices of joy; I will sing,
Yea, I will sing praises unto the Lord.
Hear O Lord, when I cry with my voice: have
Mercy also upon me, and answer me.
When Thou saidist, Seek ye my face; my heart
Said unto Thee, Thy face, Lord, will I seek.
Hide not Thy face far from me; my heart
Said unto thy servant away in anger: thou hast been my help;
Leave me not, neither forsake me, O God of my
Salvation.
When my father and my mother forsake me

> Then the Lord will take me up.
> Teach me Thy way, O Lord, and lead me in
> A plain path, because of mine enemies.
> Deliver me not over unto the will of mine
> Enemies: for false witnesses are risen up against
> Me, and such as breathe out cruelty.
> I had fainted, unless I had believed to see
> The goodness of the Lord in the land of the living
> Wait on the Lord: be of good courage, and
> He shall strengthen thine heart: wait, I say on the Lord

In other words, GOD will make your enemies your footstool. If He is for you, no matter if the world is against you. He has fought my battles many times, when my own friends had put stumbling blocks in my way. He moved them out as well as my enemies. My soul is an anchor in the LORD. I can relate when GOD's word state: "He gives me power to tread over serpents and scorpions." Stay focused on what GOD's word says. We do have power, but I had to learn how to fight back not physically, but with His word. The devil will resist you and leave you alone. I know I am a child of GOD; when you are trying to live for GOD, the devil is always trying to discourage you. It could be through your children, job, finances, or many things. The battle was not mine, for it belongs to the LORD. I had to hold my head up high, no matter what I had to go through. I had to learn to depend on GOD for everything, even when I've been lied on, talked about, and blamed for things I wasn't aware of. As GOD revealed friends and other situations, and with the help of my prayer partner, I had to change things in my life. I had to let go of the weight that was blinding me from my blessing. You see, you can be bound up and you don't even know it, but through fasting and prayer, I knew who was truly real and who wasn't real. I have this discernment and the gifts that GOD has given me to see through anyone. GOD has led me to different individuals to tell them things that they didn't know. I knew, but it had to be the LORD that gives me the words. The dreams, waking up at all times of the night praying, sometimes I used to get a little afraid to close my eyes, because I didn't know what I was going to see. I had two kids my oldest son who thought he could fool me or tell me fibs. I would tell him things GOD had shown me. It was a wake-up call for him, for being disobedient to GOD first, as well as his mother. Trials are placed in our lives to help us and make us stronger. But it is up to each one of us to want to make a change in our life; it is simple then, that you pay the price for what you do. If you sow bad seeds, you reap bad seeds. You sow good seeds, you will reap good seeds. We all have sins and have come short of the glory of GOD. We all have trials, grief hard to bear, and temptations, but carry everything to GOD in prayer. I believe in reverence to GOD. It is not the will of GOD that His people should be weighted down. He does not tell us that in being a Christian, there are no dangers in our path. He knows there are trials and dangers; we have to pay a price in order to follow him, but, our reward is everlasting life. Let nothing hinder you. Make every effort to keep open the communication between God and your soul. By being faithful, this will help me to learn more about GOD's word, and what he expects of my life. How can I become a better Christian to help a lost soul? Prayer is so powerful that it can move mountains in your life. Those that go earnest and anxious to reap all the benefits they can gain. "Now unto him that is able to do exceeding abundantly above all that we ask or think, accordingly to the power that worketh in us." (Ephesians 3:20) The assurance is broad and unlimited. When I did not receive all the things I had asked for, at the time I asked, I still believed that GOD hears and that He will answer my prayers. We are so erring and shortsighted that we sometimes ask for things that would not be blessings for us or bring that which would be for our highest good; that which we ourselves would desire if, with vision divinely enlightened, we could see all things as they really are.

When our prayers seem unanswered, we are to cling to the promise, a while and your answers will surely appear, then we will receive the blessings we need most. GOD is too wise to err, and too good to withhold any good thing from them that walk uprightly. But, do not fear to trust Him, even though you haven't seen immediate answers to your prayers. Humble yourself, acknowledge GOD in everything; through sincere prayer we are brought into connection with the mind of the infinite. Take to Him everything that perplexes the mind. Nothing is too great for him to bear, for he holds up the world. He rules over all the affairs of the universe, nothing is too small for Him to notice for His eyes are on a tiny sparrow, surely those same eyes are on you! There is no chapter in our experience too dark for Him to read. There is no perplexity too difficult for Him to unravel. JESUS is the answer; He will reach deep down to pick us up. No problem is too hard for Him to resolve, no mountain is too high for JESUS to climb. He will be there for us right on time. Acceptance helped me to deal with life as it really is not as I dreamed or hoped it would be. It enabled me to put my confidence in God and I realized that when our questions go unanswered, our

Tillie Hogans

problems unresolved, and our hopes delayed, we can cease depleting our spiritual energy on those things. We can depend on God and then work positively toward those things we can change with God's help. Contentment is a daily battle knowing that God in us strengthens us for every challenge that we are faced with. It is not how big you problems are, but how big your God is.

Early Age

At my early age I did not understand especially when it came to not using my right hand.
I always wonder out of six kids why I was the one to get so sick?
Until I realized I was special, for I was the one God picked.
There were times I would cry and wanted to be all-alone.
But I would always carry in my heart a spiritual song.
My mother didn't know what I was going through.
The hurts and pains deep within only God knew.
I lost my father at an early age
God plucked his flower but I knew he was saved
I know I missed his presence, but I know he had to go on
One day soon, I will be joined to You in our Heavenly home.
My mother is so pretty and neat
We never went to bed without anything to eat.
I love you, mom, there is no one else like you
I know God sent me to you
You all been so sweet and I love you
Too
I like to say my Lord's prayer
Jesus loves me and He cares
Touch my two children and Family with the Anointing for not to be the same
Bless them in Jesus name.

Tillie Hogans

At an early age of my childhood, I was afraid to face the world. I did have my ups and downs, but through it all, I can say that I was brought up in the best family life. I like to elaborate on my mother because she was, and still is the best mom anyone could ever want. Losing my father at an early stage was devastating to me. I went through so much pain and hurt not having my daddy around, but I had to realize that he wasn't coming back, and I needed to get on with my life. My mother did an excellent job raising seven kids without her deceased husband.

There were times as a child that I had so much hurt inside of me; I preferred to be any of my sisters beside myself. Once, I blamed my mother for my illness, but I felt terrible because she didn't have anything to do with my illness. When my father passed away many years ago, I was dealing with the grief from my father also. I appreciate my mother for caring and going out of her way to make me a happy, normal little girl. I didn't know how to handle my fears at times. Even though it was easy for me to blame others, my experiences were testing tools to get a grip on my life. Sometimes, I had to practice what I'd learned about trusting God, following your heart, and honoring yourself to grow and to believe in God's word. I could honestly say God brought me a mighty long way. I was always determined in doing anything to help myself. I was limited in a few things for instance, tying my shoes with one hand and carrying my books getting on the bus. My sisters and brothers would take turns in helping me.

Of course, my grandmother played an important role in my life and my aunt Betsy also. There was not anything that she didn't do to help my mother. She raised three of my sisters. I was back and forth from my mother to her.

I call my family a blessed family from GOD because I knew his grace and mercy was always with us. I was raised up in church, Sunday school, and Bible School. I was a very sharp individual in school; I constantly stayed on the honor roll because I didn't like for anyone to exceed me. With my disability, I felt that I shouldn't let anything get in the way of my accomplishments. If you label yourself as a loser then you are a loser. A loser never wins, but a winner will never lose, because every time you fall, you will constantly come back twice as successful. Because, I was constantly labeling myself, until I had learned to love others and myself. I looked at my mistakes and let go of judgments, and of my disabilities within myself. I focused on accepting myself and appreciating myself acknowledging that I am precious to God's sight and I was being honored and loved just as I am. I would reach out beyond my usual boundaries and catch a sense of how much more I was challenged than others. I had seen that whatever it may seem to be, I am still a child of God, God didn't give me spirit of fear, yet He gave me a spirit of power, of love and of self-discipline. Power to stand firm and motivate others to continue to be in God's presence as we keep out spiritual path. I am the pilot of my own life. Your life goes in the direction of your vision and your thoughts. You make changes in your life. Uncomfortable situations present us with choices. We should have the courage to trust God's presence, in the midst of our pains, in spite of our weaknesses. He will accept us for who we are as a person.

I was different from the other six children, not because I had polio, but because I had a mark on my life from GOD. I would always read my bible at times while the others would go to a party or elsewhere. I would stay tucked right under mother and grandmother. I would pray all the time for GOD to heal me, and I thought because I got a red cloth in the mail from a minister that it would heal me and I would always question GOD why me? Why not my other sisters and brothers?

During my school years, going into the first grade I was very afraid. I didn't know how my fellow schoolmates would react towards me. I hated myself. I didn't know if I would be picked on because of my ability to use just one arm. I didn't know if the teachers would treat me different. All these fears had me afraid of school. However, it turned out different than I had imagined. One special teacher, Ms. Dorothy Paul, took a lot of time with me. She would take me on trips with the other students; however, I always felt ashamed of my arm, and I would try to hide my hand, never wanting to wear short sleeves, only long sleeves.

I was a smart student, but I wanted to be like the other kids. I could not understand why I was the one in the family to catch polio. I would always question God, why me? I had to wear those black and white shoes. I did all I could to tear them up, but it was hard.

I lost my daddy when I was in the second grade. That put me in a painful state of mind. I held a lot of anger in my heart that no one knew. My mother Ruth had to raise seven kids without a husband but my grandmother, Osselean was always helping my mother with the children. They both worked hard to keep food and clothes for us. I felt we were a blessed family from God. We always had so much of everything. We seemed to have more than other families that only had two or more children and a nice home to live in. I couldn't understand how my mother and grandmother could do it.

God's Miracles in My Life

From the first grade up to the sixth grade, I wanted to be one of my sisters; it didn't matter which one, I just still couldn't accept myself. During my sixth grade year, I had to go back to the hospital in Pensacola for more therapy. I stayed there for six months using different exercise equipment. I know it was a difficult time for my mother, especially with me going back and forth to make sure I got the proper care and to correct my walking and sometimes even my behavior. I didn't make it easy for her. I never talked back to my mother and I was a good child but I blamed her for my illness and it wasn't fair. My mother and other family members were very faithful in coming to see me on the weekend while I was in the hospital. It would never fail they would always shower me with gifts. I didn't like going without underwear on and my mother would make sure she brought me what I wanted. The staff in the hospital was very nice to me. I pretty much always had my way it seems I had a light inside that drew people closer to me. I met this friend named Solomon while I was at my stay there. He was a very handsome young boy. He would always come and visit me in my room and we would go to the lounge to watch together. Patients were allowed to go there. I couldn't understand what was wrong with him; all I remember is that his tongue was purple. We would play games together and I really thought highly of him. He was very special to me. One day Solomon didn't come to my room to get me and I waited all day. I felt something was wrong. One of the nurses came into my room and told me Solomon had died. I felt that I had lost my best friend, and it made me so sad. I got so down and out that it seemed like staying there at the hospital would never be the same. I wanted to go home, because I looked forward to see him every day. It was times like this, I didn't want to eat, all I could think of was what happened to my friend and why he died? I had to find another friend. Although I knew, no one could ever take his place. I would wake at night and cry, because I missed Solomon so much.

Sometimes it bothered me to see children with problems and handicaps. Some parents would not come to see their children. I would feel sad for them. I would always wonder why parents would turn against their own child because of his or her disability? One particular child didn't have a nose. I did see his grandfather visit him. But, it just amazed me to actually see what some children had to go through in life. My heart always has gone out for kids and elders; I can relate to being the out cast of the family even though I wasn't treated that way. This gave me a new outlook on life that I was going to strive to make something out of life. I stayed there three months of my year in the sixth grade. After leaving there, I went back to school where I stayed on the honor roll. I stride so hard to maintain good grades in all my classes. It was times when I would pass my graded papers, around to some classmates.

During the summer, my Aunt Betsy would send for me to visit her when school was out. We had a good relationship and I felt that she was my mother too. She would buy my school clothes. She was like a mother to me, because she only had one son, David, and to her, I was like a daughter. I knew she wanted more children especially a little girl. But God knows what is best for you. My uncle was so dirty, I didn't put anything past him. For many years I had fear about men because of things that happened in my early years. I never was a disobedient fast child who would flirt to boys or men. I was quite a shy person who always wanted to make something out of life. I felt he should have been a father figure to me, since I lost my father at a young age. No one knows the hurt and pain I carried within because of my uncle. I felt I was physically imprisoned. Yet, I had the love of God, so I must try to forgive him even until his death. I can truly say I forgave him, because when he died it didn't bother me one bit. I would say to myself maybe my Aunt Betsy could live a good life for God knowing that she can find peace within. She lived a long time after his death but my aunt was very sick. She was diagnosed with cancer, and she kept it from us. She was saved. Sleep on, my aunt, you fought a good fight. I would like to dedicate this poem to you, Aunt Betsy and to my grandmother who passed a week after my aunt.

Tillie Hogans

Sleep on

Though you didn't deserve the heartache and the
pains you went through;
Because you both were so precious to me;
Yet, I won't forget all the good memories of you;
When you were both sick, you never would let on to
it;
But the smiles on your face made me strong;
Sleep On…Sleep On…
You fought a good fight;
I know your souls are resting day and night;
When I think of you, my tears begin to fall;
God's spirit looks on me through the eyes of all;
I missed the talks and the laughs we once shared;
Losing you both was hard for me to bear;
Sleep On…Sleep On…
You fought a good fight, and the victory you've
won…
I like to sing this song well done,
Well done…
You've been so faithful
Sleep On…Sleep On…
Grandmother & Aunt Betsy I know you will rise On
God's throne.

I could talk to Aunt Betsy about anything, no matter how bad I thought the situation was. I shared a lot of things with her about myself. It was one particular time when I had a bladder infection and she took me to see a doctor. I was a very shy person at this time. This doctor was examining me and I wondered why he was touching my breast but I said to myself maybe it wasn't anything, but one thing after another happened. He started kissing me in my mouth. What really devastated me was when he took his private out. I immediately got up and put on my clothes and ran out crying to my Aunt Betsy. She wanted to know what was wrong with me. I told her and she was upset with the head of staff. He ended up getting fired. This trauma made me afraid of male physicians. I was afraid of going for annual exam from then on. I was almost rape by some one that society had always taught us to trust. I was sixteen years old, this taught me not to be vulnerable to people in higher position.

I met nice gentlemen through my cousin but I always had that fear within me, and I wasn't interested in a relationship at all. We had Bible study at my cousin's house. I had met many spiritual friends there during my stay.

I didn't care too much for my uncle because he was so mean and hateful to my aunt. He would push her down the stairs and beat her. The only time he would stop was when he saw me cry. He would always call me the pretty girl and ask me why I stayed up under my Aunt Betsy all the time. Every time my aunt would go somewhere I would go with her, because my instinct told me he was not to be trusted. At times I would go across to the store and he would wait for me until I got back. One day my aunt went off and he told me I couldn't go. I developed a hatred for him. There were times when I would go and stay with my grandmother on my father's side to get away from him. He tried to rape me that day and Aunt Betsie's son, David, saved me. Those two couldn't get along at all and almost got into a fight. I told my aunt what he had tried to do and she said that she knew it was hard on me. She thought I was very brave to come and tell her. I hated my uncle. He was on a breathing machine and he was a bad diabetic patient. I hated him so much that I wanted to pull the plug so he could die. My aunt would let me go visit my other cousins and grandmother more after that happened. I was afraid to tell my mother back home, because I knew what she would do; she would never let me go back to visit my Aunt Betsy. So I kept this anger and hatred inside of me. I cared too much for my aunt to hurt her and embarrass her by telling my family. I didn't understand him because she was so pretty and I wished I was her. While I was there during the summer, Al Green, the super star was going to be there in concert. My aunt took me down town and let me get my hair done and bought me whatever I wanted to wear. I was so excited that I couldn't wait until the weekend. The day of the concert you couldn't tell me I wasn't looking good. My cousin picked me up and we went there. They laughed at me so much because I was infatuated with him. My aunt wanted me to meet her attorney and I went with her for an appointment to see him. I didn't know she had been telling him about me. I had a huge crush on men with nice texture of hair and fair complexion. When I saw him I was about to melt but I was so shy. He was a young attorney, too, and the kind of guy I would like to spend my life with, but I was only in the eleventh grade, and he was six years older than I was. I knew summer was almost over. I didn't pursue him, but I couldn't understand why my aunt wanted me to date him. I wouldn't go out with him for lunch, but that was because of fear I had during that terrible ordeal. I wouldn't let go of my fear and would push anyone who tried to get close to me away. During one of my summer months, I worked on Eglin Air Force Base and I met a nice airman that I cared a lot about. Although, the problem was they deceived many girls, because they would hide their wedding rings to pretend they were single. The place I worked gave me access to information that would tell me everything about a person. My friend, McHoward, was truthful to me; even though I did stand him up several times. He even proposed to me because he was leaving Fort Walton, Fl and going back to Oklahoma. I knew that I was about to finish the twelfth grade and I needed to proceed in continuing my education. Also the fact that I was too young to get married, and I needed to find myself and see what direction I was headed made me turn him down. I wanted to be somebody and make something out of my life. I have always wanted to be independent and do for myself. I did not want no one feeling sorry for me. Even though I did a lot of that myself, it was time for me to grow up and face reality. I was a smart girl, and I knew that I could be whatever I wanted to be if I just did it.

After I finished school, my mother had a hard time letting me go. She was very protective of me. She would always prepare different dishes, if I didn't like what she cooked. I was hardly disciplined, but when I did, it was for the tedious things. Once, I hit my sister in the head with a coca cola bottle because she wet me with a water hose. I even tried to commit suicide many times. I almost swallowed pills but my mother found out and literally beat them out of me. I would get mad and stay in my room and wouldn't eat for days. When she would leave and I was alone then I would sneak to eat other that those things I was a good child. I like cleaning up. My grandmother would let me clean her entire house when she went to work. There wasn't anything I couldn't do. Some things would be a little hard, but I always accomplished whatever it was I tried to do. I stayed on the honor roll at school. The school was desegregated during my last two years as a junior. It was hard because there were many fights at first but it eventually began to calm down. I still maintained good grades through the twelfth grade. I had teachers asking me are you going to make a one hundred on your test today? I would always say yes. I didn't want anyone to top me, because this was a challenge for me.

    I was a very timid individual and a peculiar one, too. While my sisters would go out to dances, I would very seldom go. I mostly stay around my mother and grandmothers, reading my Bible. I would get things in the mail from various people. Once I received an estranged mail about a red prayer cloth. I sent my money in and I received it back through the mail. I actually thought this prayer cloth would heal me. I was upset after I found out it didn't work. I wasn't aware at the moment until later part of my adulthood that I had many of gifts from God. I would see things as a child and it would have come to pass. I experienced seeing death and it happened with someone close in my family.

    During my prom in the eleventh grade, I had two dates but of course I had to tell one of the guys no. I ended up going with the son of one of my teachers. It was funny because one of my closest friends ended up on a double date with us. I was afraid, because the majority of the guys wanted to go elsewhere but I didn't let that happen. I have always demanded respect for myself.

After graduation, I went to St. Petersburg, and that was a big step for me. I had some relatives there that I visited and stayed with sometimes on the weekend. I also met an older man who worked at the school, and who would send me love letters almost every other day. Sometimes there was money in the envelope. Of course my roommates and I would spend the money, but I wasn't interested in this person at all. When I would tell him, it seemed that he wouldn't get the picture and I don't like to take advantage of anyone. You know how it is when you're away from home and your money runs out. He kept continually sending me money even after I told him to stop. He never stopped, but I can truly say that he never tried to approach me in any way. He did give me respect and I thanked him for that reason.

I learned how to bowl while I was there on the weekend, and that's what I enjoyed the most besides shopping. I stayed in the dormitory where I met many associates and made a few friends with a few. I worked in a Goodwill store, where I learned different skills. Everything was going along fine, until I met one girl named Inez. She was very nice but I wondered why she liked to follow me when I took my shower at night and in the morning. That was very strange to me but I didn't think much about it. She asked me one day would I like to go home with her for the weekend to Tampa. Of course, I said yes and I was very excited about going until one day when we were eating in the cafeteria and she got mad and was getting ready to fight another girl because she was sitting by me. From that point on I knew this girl was funny, and I stopped being her friend. I know God has always watched over me and He is real in my life. I got over that problem, and then I got pushed up against the wall by one guy because I didn't like him. What made me leave St. Petersburg was that I had one night class and we were watching a film. The teacher I had came by and sat next to me. He started touching me on my leg and feeling me. I was so upset. I knew it was time for me to leave from St. Petersburg and I did. I went back home to DeFuniak Springs. Some people put out lies that I was pregnant. It seems that the harder I tried to better myself, the more steps behind I took. MY Uncle Floyd on my father's side came home from New York and took me back with him. My mother was very sad this time. She told me that I could not go but I packed my clothes and left anyway. After looking back, when we were leaving, I saw her standing there crying. It made me feel sad. I wasn't trying to hurt her, but all I could think of was doing something with my life. All I wanted was for her to give me a chance to find myself, because one of many favorite quotes "A quitter will never win and a winner will never quit." I went on to Queens, New York, where I was enrolled in a Federal Assistant School and finished. I learned how to get around on a train and bus to go downtown in New York City. My friend and I would go to movies. I was always attracted to men of high authority and I had a big crush on this pastor at the church I attended. His wife was deceased and I knew we could have a commitment with each other. I really cared a lot about him. Every time he tried to make a move on me I would avoid him as though he wasn't there. I couldn't understand why I did that. I knew I didn't want to be hurt and I wasn't going to develop any trust in him or anyone else until I got myself together. I wanted education, a good job, and to be independent. I knew that I was capable of reaching my expectations of myself. I wasn't going to accept any handouts from anyone. I didn't want anyone feeling sorry for me because of my disability. That was one of the reasons I had to leave my mother. I couldn't see myself living with her and her taking care of me. I needed to face reality myself. If I fall, let me get up and try again; I could have gotten a check for the rest of my life, but I turned it down. I wasn't going to let any kind of government assistance take care of me. I didn't let anything or anyone get in my way. I wanted to have accomplishments in my life. I wasn't going to put a limit on what I could or could not do. I would often cry and I had developed a low self-esteem. Some parts of me inside would not allow me to give me, no matter how bad things and the situations seemed.

I knew God played an important role in my life. He is always there working out problems and situations when I didn't know what my next step was going to be. His words tell us to be still and know that He is God. I can tell you He does not need help. He has guided me and protected me during some difficult times.

Before leaving New York, I did finish my courses and I was proud of myself. I didn't care for the snow or the city either, because it's too fast for me. You know, in a big city, people do not care for anyone. I have seen men lying in the street dying, and people would walk around them like it didn't matter to them and that would bother me. Also, I realized that the city wasn't for me, and I didn't want to live there. I wanted to go back home, but I was afraid to hurt my uncle's feelings because he was so good to me. He helped me when I felt like I was in a crisis. I felt his wife had become jealous of me and that I had worn out my welcome. A few people were invited over when they had a get together. It seems that everyone was always attracted to me. Also, my aunt's mother's boyfriend, who was a lot younger then her, wanted to date me. I was not going to let that happen and I didn't, even though they got suspicious about him. I knew it was time for me to leave. During my stay she had got so jealous she would do my hair and cut it. That made me so mad. One day I had enough when my uncle got home he found me crying and I told him I was ready to go back home. That's when he made reservations for me to go back home. He didn't want me to leave but he wanted me to be happy. After arriving back home, I had a short stay.

My classmate and I decided to go to Tallahassee and attend school and it is currently where I reside today. We got an apartment across from the college and vocational school. My roommate and I were making a decision about whether or not we were going to take up a trade or go to Tallahassee Community College. I wanted to capture what I really wanted to be or do with my life, even though I had a low self esteem about myself. God plays important roles in my life and always getting me through problems and situations when I didn't even know myself. I assure you if you put God first in you life ask for His protection and guidance, your life will be different. I'm not saying you are not going to have problems but my life depends on faith in Him. We both decided to take up a trade at Lively VoTech, childcare and bookkeeping. In the process of finishing the course I met a man named Mr. Aaron Gaines. He helped me get a job while going to be, and helped me in whatever way he could. I will never forget him. He is deceased, but I like to honor him and any others who helped me in accomplishing my goals. Who was there for me, and anyone who had faith in me I sincerely thank you. After I completed my course, I interned at a nursery, I really love children. It was very exciting to see babies grow up into little toddlers while I was watching and playing with them.

I loved GOD at an early age but didn't fully understand exactly what my purpose on earth was on earth. I've foreseen things that had already happened to me as I reading my adulthood. For instance, I saw myself driving and getting a car while lying on the bed at my early age. I would wonder how this was going to happen. I can't drive with the use of only one hand. But, you see, that taught me nothing is impossible with GOD and He is real. There were many things that came before me and it happened just like I saw it. As a child, I had fights with my sisters. I never had problems with my oldest sister and oldest brother. Sometimes my oldest sister would fuss at me about bothering her clothes, but it didn't do any good; I would still slip and wear what I thought looked good on me unless I was caught. I did my chores like anyone else in the family. I also would clean my grandmother's house all by myself. Sometimes my sisters might help out, but I enjoyed doing housework. I know if it had not been for Him I would have died at an early age. I learned many people fight their good rather than accepting it, and that was me. I foolishly thought that I couldn't accept the good, nor should I be asking for it. Such attitudes are no part of the child of a king. Do not burden yourself with such false ideas, feeling sorry for yourself. This only blocks our good from getting through us; in the process, nothing is too good to be true, nothing is too wonderful to happen. Nothing is too good to last; it is our Father's good pleasure that we receive it. My childhood going to school was not so bad at all. I really wasn't bullied like I imagine in my mind. I did have a fight with several classmates and we ended up best friends. Sometimes it takes defending yourself to anyone that tries to give you a hard time. When they find out you're not afraid that's when they back off. Even though I was frightened of fighting, the fact is that you have to do things that you don't like to do, either to win their friendship or to go your separate ways.

Too many of us spend time resisting, resenting, and mentally fighting the people in our world. If you do not like your world and the people in it, you can change it by changing your consciousness by changing your thoughts and feelings about problem people. It is not good to be with all types of people that have a strong bond on your life. At an early age that's very important task, the company you keep labels you, and I know it has an impact on your life. Everyone does not want to make something out of life; they are placed there to hinder you. We have some people that have often been conditioned to expect less than the best in life, there by settling for and living in limitations. We learn the unlimited truth about GOD's goodness and man's availability because that is one of the things I can say never put Man before GOD or anything not even my own family. He should always be first not in the middle or last. God is the source of all our good. He will never leave you or forsake you. God will use people as channels for a blessing to you. He will put people in your life for your personal growth. Failures are not bad to go through, when you take falls and gain from it. It makes you better; I accomplished many goals during my early age. When I began to experience hurt, anger, and fear, it gradually moved the obstacles out of my way, and fed positive things in my mind that said "I am somebody. I belong to God, and He has a purpose in life for me." I studied hard and applied myself to make good grades. Needless to say, I didn't let anyone stop me or get in the way of achieving anything I set out to do. I was in the Glee Club talent shows, and I won a spelling bee contest; I maintained my place on the honor roll from elementary up to high school. Drama class sweetheart, I was respected by my peers and classmates, overall by everyone. I thank God for instilling in me the personality to love everyone. It's like I attract people, no matter where I go, or what place I may be. People get attached to me. We all have received a gift from God of growth and expansion. By understanding the process of growth, it is easy to accept your good and expand it more quickly. Once I realized and put my foot on the inner path and learned about using the power within me as a tool for my good, my growth began to accelerate, to help me recognize and understand the phases I shall accomplish, so my growth can be unaccompanied by pain. There will be trying times in your process of growth, but it is most important too, that when many of us give they get no further. I never was the one that would say I couldn't do; to me that's an excuse, and I feel that your success depends on God and yourself. Because I wanted to make good grades in school and be active, I didn't allow my handicap to get in my way. I always felt that if you could do it, then do so. I always wanted to be the best at whatever I did. It may have been difficult at times. Sometimes I used another way of getting it done, but I didn't use that for an excuse for not doing things. I had that intuition to go on and strive. I have to succeed at different levels in my life, let patience have its perfect work that ye may be perfect and entire, lacking in nothing (James 1:4)

I had to have self-determination, having trusted in myself by finding something that I love to do and becoming very proficient at doing it. From elementary through High school, I worked hard to achieve and stayed on the honor roll. I was not going to accept less. I was valued for what I did as well as for who I was, and in recognizing my own falling into the old habit of putting myself down, I had to realize that I cannot run from my problems. I realized that I had to be strong and hold on to my dreams and not let whether you believe it or not matter to me. Your thoughts and words determine your reality. When I started changing my mind, my life began to change. I wanted to do better. You are going to find obstacles. The obstacles in my path were to make me stronger. No matter how difficult it was, I still had to stand and wait on God. One thing I can say, it will make you or break you. I knew I was doing right in the sight of God because my trials were coming left and right and I knew that I was special in God's sight. The harder your trials the better person you become.

God helps those who want to be able to help themselves. You can make a difference in what you want in life. We have good times and bad times, but don't let bad times get the best of you. Even in bad situations, there are good that comes from them. Every trial has made me wiser, stronger and helped me get even stronger for the next storm. Seeking and overcoming the obstacles that life presents constantly impelled me upward. You want to develop, and grow, to expand the good that is born within you. It is a part of the divine nature. Some people have it harder than others. I was the one that was picked out to go through suffering within my spirit, because God knew that they could not handle life's challenges. You are forced forward on the path of growth into maturity, depth, and understanding. God's purpose for my life is growing in dark periods, as well as in the happier ones. When your life takes a new direction that is a part of your growth. You are where you are that you may learn, and as you learn, the trials which any obstacle has for you. The obstacles pass away and give you other circumstances and surroundings.

My goal is to enlighten people about God, to let them know there is nothing impossible in anyone's life that He can't change. Writing this book was a big enchantment for me, although it was not easy to write about myself, because it brought things to light, and the fear in my life that's so deep that I just kept it bound up inside of me for a long time. I felt that my book was assurance that would turn people's life around to achieve the goal of my life. I had to want to be somebody and have plans and expectations for these plans to be fulfilled through faith in God and believing in yourself. Because, if you don't know it by now, it starts with your self—first! Obviously, it would be wise to contemplate in what direction we are moving or rather, in what directions our minds are taking us. My goals are to help people, especially the lives of children and elders. I always said when I make it financially how I wanted to help so many people and especially my family. I always dream of having the best. That's been my weakness is buying clothes and new furniture. Also, my goal to grow spiritually and continually in the Lord, to witness to people and to be a light for them; what I mean is that we have many people who are in the dark and have not found the way out because of these conditions and situations. It has become their enemy. Everybody is somebody. I really would like to reach many young souls; to me that is where it starts. I see so many of our young ones just throwing their lives away, and it bothers me. I have always had an interest in children. I would like to reach as many as I can. I want to help the homeless, come up with a program for housing, to promote jobs for them, and get them somewhat in a mind frame of wanting to help themselves.

A person can be what they determine to be. He can be a survivor or he can be a quitter. No matter how hard you try to help someone, you will always find those that don't want to be helped. I truly believe what a man thinks becomes a part of him. We may or may not stay with setting goals and making changes in our lives that we feel will help us, but they give us something to work towards as well as provide a measure for greater our achievements. The most important resolution that I made for those years was to be the very best I could be and to work hard in making those goals happen. We can live in the present and not in the past or the future. Because we know this, we can live fully and completely. There is no guarantee that we will reach every goal, but we can let God's love be the motivation for all that we do. I live in my divine capabilities by having the confidence to meet each challenge with faith. Whenever I come to a turning point in life, there is a new beginning for me, I meet it with faith, because there is a divine plan at work in my life. I know that every new beginning will contain something of meaning and value for me. I am making progress in my growing awareness of my own spirituality. God is constantly preparing me for my life. My faith is in God's hand and no matter how tiny my faith may seem at times, it is my unbreakable lifeline of awareness to the greatness of God. Although I may or may not consider myself materially wealthy, I know that money and possessions do not guarantee happiness and fulfillment in my life as in other matters. I know that God blesses me with the abundance of spirit. I understand that every ending holds the promise of a new beginning.

Tillie Hogans

Deep within

As I walk alone this journey
Experiencing the birth of growth deep within
Abiding God's words in my heart and in my life
Knowing that I can call on Jesus, for he is my best friend
Though the pain that falls from above the sky
When struggles come I wonder why
Sometimes my trials were like a ship on a stormy sea
But the waves were so peaceful and calm I knew what Jesus meant to me

Jesus is the road sign, not the designation
Through his power and love I learned to be patient
We sometimes never know what we are going to go through
But it's only a test. Jesus loves me and I know he do.

His spirit dwelled deep within my soul
He always with me as I'm traveling this road
His arm stayed open and always welcomes you to come in.
Obey his voice the heavenly gate is open
But you got to be born-again…

God's Miracles in My Life

I was dating this guy; we got engaged, but he was going to college in Madison, Florida. He was originally from Valdosta, Ga. My roommate and I went in different directions. She left and went to Detroit, and I moved in with my sister who had just moved up here and had a four-year scholarship to FSU. She was my baby sister. We got along so good; I could always talk to her. After two months of staying with my sister, I found out I was pregnant by the guy I was dating. He wanted to get married and move to Madison, so I did. He was very good to me but was very jealous. I could never understand why! He didn't want any other men talking to me. We had big fights about that. It was almost time for me to have the baby when I moved back to Tallahassee with my sister Brenda. I was so afraid; I was not ready for a baby. I asked myself how could I raise a baby with the use of only one hand. On January 14, 1978, I had a seven-pound, seven-ounce baby boy. I had an easy delivery, I had my baby naturally. My baby was so pretty; he looked like a precious girl. I knew I had to be a mother to my baby because he didn't ask to be here. My sister Brenda was a big help to me, I started putting in applications for state jobs one after another, every time I would put in one I would get rejection letters. I was getting depressed but I kept praying, and still continued to put in for jobs. One day I received a call from Bonnie Everton from the Department of Revenue. She scheduled an interview with me. I went and I felt nervous about it, but she said that she had forty applicants and she would let me know. I was about to give up when she called and told me I got the job and I could start work June 6, 1978. I was so happy; I knew my prayers had been answered. My next problem was who was going to keep my baby. This couple named Mr. & Mrs. Zales Maddox came into my life, wanted to keep my child for me during the week and will bring my child back on the weekend. I didn't want to stay away from my child that long but at the time, I didn't have a choice. I knew the couple was a Godsend. If he had a doctor's appointment, they would take him for me. I had a way to and from work; although I didn't have a car at that time, everything was looking like it was falling in place and I knew that it was a miracle from God, and He had answered many prayers for me. My friend would come up on the weekends and sometimes during the week to see the baby and me.

Raising my son was very hard. He was very smart as a child in school. But He always wanted to be the clown of the class. I felt it was because at his early age, I would give him math problems to do before going to class everyday. His work wasn't a challenge for him, I had a conference once with his teachers and they would tell me that he didn't have to study like the average students and would still produce the same accurate answer. I sometimes wondered if I was too strict on Ryan, my son, because I knew I was very particular about everything he did.

He had his chores to do because I wanted my place tidy and clean all the time. I would even fuss at Ryan if his room was a little out or order. I didn't spare the rod with him. I knew a child would be a child. Although I didn't play when it came to respecting your parents. In raising my child, because I didn't want to have anything else to do with his father, I had to play the roles of both parents. I would do it all over again. I know I gave him the best; yet, sometimes I worried about whether I was too hard on him. I know I can be a difficult person at times, and sometimes I found myself being an over-protective mother. I was afraid of who my child was playing with in the neighborhood. I carried this fear inside for a while, even up until Ryan was older. I didn't want my child getting dirty while he was playing with other children. If he did, immediately he had to take a bath and put on clean clothes.

His father had got orders to go in the army and I had to make up my mind if I wanted to marry him or not. But deep within me I was not ready for that. Sometimes in your younger age you think that you are in love but it's not always so. I prayed to God about whether this was the right man for me. Although part of me wanted to say yes, the other part said no. I know I had high expectations for myself about what I wanted to accomplish out of life. I always wanted to be that independent person. There was more in life than just being married. My friend wanted me to go with him that weekend to see his family in Valdosta, Georgia, before he went into the Army, so I did. We stayed with his brother and wife. He seemed overprotective of me; you know how sometimes you feel like you are smothered, that's the way I felt. He and his brother and wife went out to club that Saturday night; I never was the one to drink but sodas. I was having fun, that's what I thought, until I was asked to dance by someone else. I didn't feel that it was a problem, because he was out dancing with someone else. That's when the problems began. That is when I began to see the pictures. Oh you can dance with someone but I can't, I do not think so. He got an attitude with me. The rest of that night and going back to Tallahassee on that Sunday we did not say two words to each other, his cousin came back with us. After arriving back he went on in the room and his cousin and I carried on a conversation without him, when all of a sudden he came in and slapped me, and his cousin made him to leave me alone. I knew that was God letting me know that he was not the one and that was my answer. I cried and told him to get out and take everything he had with him; I took the ring off and tore up pictures we had taken together. He begged, cried and pleaded with me not to leave him, but it was over with me. I didn't want him anywhere in my sight. I thought if he gets mad at me about this little petty thing, what would he do if a bigger problem existed. I have always said that I would leave a man if he ever hit me, because the next time could be more severe. I didn't regret the decision that the mercy of God had to let me experience. To me, that was a wake-up call. My friend kept trying to convince me to take him back, he kept saying that if I ever leave him he would kill me, over and over until I had to go and get a restraining order out on him. I also had my child's name changed back into my last name. I told the judge I don't want any child support from him, all I want is for him to leave me alone. I began to develop a hatred for him; I couldn't stand to see him or look his way. He tried to get on my good side by buttering up my mother and grandmother by bringing things over for my child. My family would try to keep it from me that those gifts were from him because they knew how I felt, and I wouldn't accept anything from him. It was hard for me to raise my child by myself, but God saw me through. My child always had the best, my God made ways out of no way. He will fix it for you when you lean and depend on Him. He brought me through with so many people He's placed in my life to help me. One of my brothers wanted me to give my child to him, but I wouldn't because that was my responsibility. I would work on an eight-hour job every day, go to FSU

(Florida State University) for management courses, and stay up almost all night studying. My child never went hungry; he stayed clean. I made sure of that. I was the type of person who likes being organized and planning ahead. I would get my child's and my things out at night when he was with me. His God parents Barbara and Zayres Maddox help me out so much, because they knew I wanted to attend college also. They would always get him for me; most of the time, I wouldn't get him until the weekend. Another thing about me is because I was raised that way, I like my place to be spotless all the time. I couldn't stand to see anything not in place. Many people were amazed about me and would question me how could I keep my place so clean. I thank God for my family that even though I lost my father at an early age, my mother and grandmother did an excellent job with seven children. I know I came from a blessed family. I knew I was the peculiar one out of my family, but I can say every one of my sisters and two brothers always wanted to have the best of everything. I had my ups and downs like anybody else. I knew one thing I didn't want to get involved with anyone any time soon. It seemed at times that my friend wouldn't leave me alone. I couldn't go visit my mother and grandmother. He had become close with them, and my mother would get on me about being so hateful to him. I didn't want to be that way, but I really despised him. It seemed like I couldn't help it the way I felt, I had to pray for God to remove that hatred out of my heart, because I am not a mean person. It did take some time to overcome that obstacle, but I did just like the song says it's a thin line between love and hate. All I wanted was to go forward in life. He finally gave up on me, and I felt that was the best thing he could ever do for me. I had a job, and I knew that God would make a way for me no matter how hard it might seem to me. I went through lots of fear within myself. I was frightened by the fact that I had to step out there on my own and prove to myself that I am somebody that can do or be whatever I want to be as long as I had that faith, and do not let negative feelings, struggles, and people, get in my way. I would tell myself I can do it even with my disability because everyone has something handicapped about them, whether it is a physical or a mental condition, no one is perfect but God. Every human being is special in God's sight, no matter what people and society think. I begin to move up into different job positions. I went from a clerk I to a clerk II. That's when I wanted to correct some defects that I had from the polio. I went to Gainesville to see if there was any hope for my arm, because it was just there. I didn't have any movement at all. The only thing was that I had feeling in my arm just like my normal hand. I went through my primary physician to set up an appointment for Gainesville. When I got there, they began to do many tests on my right arm to see if there was any hope. I did pass all the requirements that they had for me to do with my arm. Dr. Dell, who was my doctor, told me some of the things he could do to improve my arm. I could have my shoulder and wrist fused to give me some mobility there. Those were the options. I had to decide whether I wanted it done or not. It was my decision. I went on and told him yes, because I felt if anything could help, what could I lose? Something was better than nothing. He also told me that they would be coming up with other experimental procedures that gave me hope. I went on and had the surgery done. I stayed there in the hospital for two weeks. I had so much pain in that arm; I would cry a lot

God's Miracles in My Life

while I was there, the pain was so unbearable. I did take pain medicine but once it wore off, it was hard for me to cope with the pain. I had therapy while I was there. Everyone was so nice during my stay. I saw so many people that had gotten in bad car accidents or other aliments, which made me appreciate that, when I look over my life I could have been worse. I didn't accomplish a lot, but I knew within myself that I was not going to give up no matter how long it took. I left Gainesville; my oldest sister took me home to stay with my mother for recovery. I was out of work for a month. I went back to work where everyone was so concerned and willing that they helped me with whatever I needed. I was always a friendly, outgoing person; I never met a stranger; I can get along with anybody. There wasn't anything I would not do for people, especially children and elders. My heart always reached out; I almost lost my child, Ryan, when he was 2 years of age. While I was preparing dinner that Sunday, getting ready to go back to church, a friend of mine supposedly had been watching my son when he got in the pool at the apartment complex, I don't know how it happened. I was crying, and devastated, wondering if my child was going to live or die. The manager there gave my child mouth-to-mouth resuscitation. He starting coming to. We were rushed to the hospital by ambulance. When we got there, he was in critical condition. He was on a twenty four-hour watch. I was afraid to call my home and rest of the family but I did. I knew they were mad at me although I blamed myself but God saw us through his recovery. He stayed in the hospital for four days, and they released him to go home. I knew it was God's grace and mercy that he came out of it but I had to learn my lesson also, not depend on anybody to watch my child and I learned not to take anything for granted. I moved from were I was living because I didn't ever want to live where a swimming pool was, even though I couldn't stop accidents from happening to my child. I was very paranoid and overprotective of my child. During this stage of his growing up, I was afraid of him playing with other children and going outside to play. When school would get out, I would take him up to my mother and grandmother to keep for me until school started again. I was gradually moving up at my job to other positions. I always wanted to be friendly with everyone and wanted to be accepted by everybody. I remember at times I would take my break with coworkers who I thought were my friends, but I would see them laughing and talking about everyone, and I felt uncomfortable in their company. This one particular time I was with them I heard a voice telling me to move away from them. I was afraid not to obey the voice, so I did stop being around them. I was ridiculed and talked about, but that let me know that not everybody that you laugh and talk with is your friend. You live and you learn. The best lesson anyone can appreciate is going through trials and tribulation. I knew I was a different person; I've always walked with God. I have been through obstacles in life and I know that no one brought me out but the Lord. I have always been kind of a lonely person; I didn't care too much for being with the crowds, even when I stayed by myself most of the time. I didn't care for a lot of company visiting me. Believe me, I have gotten burned by friends too many times. We have people that just want to know your business and will pretend they really care about you. I have been hurt so much in my life, thinking I have good friends, but the strange thing I have experienced in my life is that GOD would always show me things. Sometimes

I disobeyed him and continued to be used, lied to, talked about, and mistreated by others, just to keep their friendship, until I was tired of being used, and I decided to walk closer to GOD. I wanted to better my life and my condition, so I went back to the doctor to get x-rays.

When I met someone at revenue (at my place of work), first I didn't want to be bothered and I didn't like him. I just wanted to be a friend; I had this thing for bright-skinned black men with nice curly hair. So, I didn't pursue him like that, I was interested in one person on my job, we dated until he left and moved back up north. I got involved with someone else who was involved with someone else; he was a true gentleman and treated my son and me with respect. But there were people in our business.

Even those I considered my friends were involved in my relationship. I became pregnant with my second child. I moved out of my house and moved in with him. I didn't realize I was making the biggest mistake of my life.

Diagnosis

Problem after problem started cropping up. I sold some of my things to move in with him and moved the rest there. It was fine, I thought, we moved into a nice home because I need more space for my things, he didn't mind because I was having his baby. I had to stay in the hospital for eight days, because I was diagnosed with diabetes and I had to give insulin shots to myself. My doctor thought at one point that I was having twins or a nine-pound baby because of the shape of my stomach. I had problems with one of his sisters. She told me because I wouldn't go along with her into a relationship with a married man. Then I found out all the wrong things she was doing, and she told a lot of lies. I had a conscience; I couldn't have that person's blood on my hands. Since I wouldn't go along with her, She turned on me and kept things going on between her brother and me. This one particular time, she came over to our place and I felt like I was going into labor at seven months. I would always hear a voice that always directed me to get the bible and read the 23rd Psalm, which I did, and place that verse on my stomach and the pain left, I began to pray and pray she came back the next day, the same thing happened again, so I began to read the verse again this time I prayed to GOD to not let her come back over there, and He didn't. I knew she was trying to get me to lose my baby. No one knows what I went through being in that relationship. I was so tired of carrying my child but didn't understand why I wouldn't go in labor until the doctor decided that he was doing a c-section on me. During my pregnancy, some of my co-workers and friends thought I was tripping because I told them GOD showed me I was having a girl, and she had a dimple. I'll never forget, one co-worker said to me, I want to see what GOD you serve and laughed at me. I said ok; I went out buying girl's clothing, and my friend would get mad at me. I had that much faith that GOD does things for a reason. The time came for me to go back to the hospital around six o'clock. The nurse gave me an anesthesia shot in the back. The doctor told me that I would never be able to have my child naturally. My unborn child had her hands over her face. She was seven pounds and six ounces; from then on I was not worried about my dreams anymore. Jonathan was a great provider, and he took good care of all three of us. We've been through ups & downs similar to other relationships and not once has he ever lifted a finger to hit me, although, at times there would be verbal abuse thrown between the two of us. He always was right and I was always wrong. I took blame for everything, even though I was right from the start. I was accused of dating other men behind his back, which I would never do. Jonathan was the love of my life. I prayed so much to get out of that relationship and promised my SAVIOR that I would never live with a man again before marriage. I was in a depressed state. Jonathon was trying to be a "good man" so I fell for it again. I would always fall for his act every time. I thought things were going right, but I was wrong. I felt like I could never do anything right. I pursued the relationship only for my sweet *children*, who were ten years apart. I knew I was not financially ready to be out on my own. I didn't have a key to the house. On several occasions Jonathon locked us out of our own home. Then, I would go to the department stores until I thought he had made it home. There were times when I would come home and find my clothing all out on the floor. Because, he thought I was out with other men. I would be so furious. We didn't have any communication at all.

One of my dear friends would go behind my back and lie about me to others. Although, she wouldn't confess to it, I stayed friends with her.

I went to the doctor because I was concerned about my feet and I received different opinions from two doctors stating that surgery would correct the problem.

On March 21, 1995, I went to have a major surgery on both of my feet at Tallahassee Memorial Hospital. The Doctor felt it would be too much for me, so he decided to restructure my right foot, since that was the worst one. The day of my surgery, I was so scared that I wanted to back out. I was the second patient scheduled for surgery that morning. All I remember when I was taken down to the operating room was the IV that went into my arm. Before I knew it, in a matter of seconds, I was in a deep sleep. When I woke up I asked for more covers, because I was shaking all over; even my teeth was rattling, and it was hard for me to come out of my sleep. Finally, they took me to my room, my mother and brother-in-law were there. I was in lots of pain, so the nurse brought in more medications for the pain. All I wanted to do was sleep and drink juices because my mouth stayed dry. I was a little upset because I wanted a private room but some how I didn't get one the first day. My mother had to leave to go back home in Defuniak Springs, but she told me that they would come back up on the weekend.

The second day, I did get a private room that made me feel much better, but the pain seemed like it was getting harder and harder. My third day there the nurse told me I would be transferred over to Tallahassee Memorial extended care unit that afternoon. I really didn't want to go but I had no choice. After I got there, I was back in a room with another patient, because they didn't have private rooms left. You can imagine how I felt after looking at the place. It had a smell that I couldn't cope with. I had one of my co-workers bring me some incense to put in my room. There were about four young patients and the others were old. I felt I didn't have anything to look forward to, all I could think was "Let me go home," but I knew that wouldn't happen, because I had to learn how to walk again. I had screws in my right foot with a cast up to my knee. For days, I wouldn't eat anything, until one nurse told me they would cook me whatever I liked if I would just eat, so I did. I met so many nice nurses while I was there. I'd know when it was time for the nurses to give the patients sponge baths. I let them know I wanted a bath in the morning and to be taken to the shower at night, and I would take care of myself. No matter how much pain I was in, I wanted to take my own showers. I would have therapy twice a day. It was hard and painful at first, but I learned to deal with the pain so I could hurry and go home. At times I would wake up and cry, *never take life for granted*. I can say that I was blessed when I saw patients there that were worse off than I. I was feeling sorry for them, because some couldn't do anything for themselves; that showed me that we don't know how blessed we are to have some or all of our body parts. My heart went out for many; I saw how some got mistreated because they couldn't help themselves. I lay there and wondered if that person was fed or did they get a sponge bath that day, and that really worried me. I can say I had good care.

Somehow, everyone seemed to like me. I had this therapist, Lillian Garcia, who would bring me presents, and we became very close. There were so many nurses that arranged a birthday party for me. The first thing I had to accomplish was walking up the steps with the cast on my leg. I had to complete each level before going home. I had good days and some bad days. I got so upset one day, because I was tired of being there. My sister from Pensacola and mother came up that day to see me. I felt like I couldn't stand another day in there after seeing my family gave me strength to endure a little longer. It never failed—they always brought me gifts. I can say I had some nice co-workers. Some days my work section would surprise me and bring me lunch, and we would all sit outside and have so much fun.

One special co-worker was like a mother to me. I will never forget her, Jackie Brown. If I needed anything, she would see to it that I got it. She would go out her way to buy me short sets for my therapy and give me baths from time to time. I had others who helped me, but she was special. There are so many people I want to thank GOD for, because they were there when I was going through a difficult time learning how to walk again. When I finally got my cast off, my doctor had to get the stitches out of my feet. The day it was done somehow he forgot to give me something for pain, He had the other doctor to hold me down while he got them out. I howled at the top of my lungs. I knew everybody there heard me. I never in my life experienced stitches hurting that bad; to me it was worse than having a baby.

My feet felt so numb and funny. I knew the worst was over. Now it was time for me to get out of my wheel chair and try to walk. I was so determined to walk, I did every exercise in therapy that I was told and had to do. Some days it hurt so bad that when I got back to my room, I wanted pain medicine so I could sleep and be left alone.

I got attached to many people while I was there. I had visitors all the time, even times when I wanted to be by myself. I stayed there six weeks. When it was time for me to leave, some people were sad but I was ready, especially when I discovered some of my clothes and perfumes were missing. They were taken not by my therapist, but by some of the young nurse assistants who would stay in my room all the time. I had an idea who it was but it didn't matter to me, since knew I was going home. The day I left, my therapist, Lillian packed all my clothes and perfume so nothing else would be taken. The goodbyes were sad, and I knew I would miss everyone, but I was ready to leave.

I began to walk better, and I knew that the surgery had worked for me. I didn't have a limp. I knew I was going to need my friend's help. He did just that; he was good to me and did whatever he could while I was going back and forth to the doctor. I didn't know how long it was going to take for him to go back being his old self again. I never had known what to expect from him. I sometimes feel that he was demon-possessed from day to day. What moods he would be in! I have been in and out of the relationship, but I was at a point where I couldn't take any more, and I had to do something about it. I had to step out on faith when I started looking for my own place. I left this time for good; half of the story is not told because I will get emotional and I try to block things out of my mind.

Sometimes, I wonder why some people are so cruel. Now we are fighting over who is going to get my little girl. right now she is with him majority of the time. He would do things behind my back and deliberately lie on me, but something I always reminded myself that God's word says "Vengeance is his and what goes around will come around," I thought one time I was losing my mind after the Judge gave my girl to him temporarily.

I hated him for that, but I got over the hurt and pain by praying to GOD to help me. I have prayed at times to GOD not to wake me up due to all the things I went through, but I realize it was not God's will. I know for a fact, I had a true friend who was there for me. When I was going through this, she always helped me and would be angry at how some people treated me. She always told me that different ones were going to pay for the way they treated me. But I am always nice; I finally came around and started talking to him because he would bring my child to me on the weekends. Somehow I couldn't ever trust him for what he did to me, but I had to deal with him because he was the father if my child. That's why I stayed in the relationship, because of her. She loved her daddy, and I needed help with her. There was times when he was trying to turn my daughter against me by telling her I didn't love her, feeding her all kinds of information about school. If I hadn't found out about it myself, I would be left in the dark. It would hurt me so bad. There were times when I felt I didn't have anyone in the world but GOD, but I knew He was the one I truly needed. I knew John also dealt in witchcraft, he was so wicked. At times strange things had taken place, and I didn't trust him at all. I felt like I was in bondage and I was afraid of him not bringing my child when it was time to keep her. He would have her asking me questions about different things, and I knew it was him, she was a very confused child. I wouldn't put a child through anything like that. There were times GOD would put songs in my heart and one particular song that goes like this, "GOD got his eyes on you." I would tell John that whenever he would mistreat me, "you don't know how GOD (enables) me."

Although I don't have words to express it, on February 10, 1998 I wanted to do something about my life, so I made up my mind that I was going to see if they had come up with any experimental surgery for my arm. I went to see my primary doctor to see what he thought. Of course he has always been so nice to me. He got a referral for me to go to the University of Florida Shands clinic at Hampton Oaks Hand Surgery for a follow-up and I did. He explained what

God's Miracles in My Life

he was going to do to see if I could get any used from the surgery but I had to get other tests done to see if this could happen, and if there was any hope this operation can be done on my arm. Dr. Bell gave me the orders to take back to Tallahassee to have the tested done. I went back to doctor was he and his nurses would make sure everything was arranged for me like the doctor in Gainesville had instructed. I had to go to Tallahassee Memorial Hospital, were they tested my nerves. When I had that done, it was not so pleasant, some spots were worse than others. I wanted them to hurry and finish that test. After that I was sitting and waiting to see the results. Two other doctors came in and examined my right arm and were asking me different questions. Although my feeling in my arm was always there. The doctor felt the result from the x-rays it wasn't no reason why I couldn't have the surgery done that they had requested. All plans were made through my primary care physician Dr. Wess and I was schedule to have surgery on April 14, 1998 in Gainesville. I had to be there on April 13, 1998 for my pre-op. I was very excited, because, if I could used my right hand, that would be a big step in my life. My cousin drove me there. We spent the night at the home of one of my close friends in Bunelle. I headed back to Gainesville by 9:45. On the day of my surgery, they were running a little behind. I was getting nervous sitting and waiting for it to be time for me to go. I had to lie on my side for the Doctor to perform my surgery; they took a muscle out of my back on the right side and placed in my right arm. When I awakened, I was in a lot of pain. I never in my entire life had experienced pain like this. Because I laid on my left hand during surgery I couldn't move my fingers and I got so afraid that tears were running down my face. I started questioning the nurses about why I could barely use my hand. They thought that it wasn't anything to worry about, but to me, that fear was there. It was hard for me to deal with this. All I could think of is if lose the use of that hand, what was I going to do? That meant I couldn't use either hand, but I began getting all the use back. I spent only one night in the hospital; they were going to keep me for a couple of days, but the doctor did not see any complications so they released me and I went back home to Tallahassee. I had drainage from my back—blood kept going into this bag. At the time my niece was staying with me, and she helped me out so much. She would empty the bag, bathe me, and keep the house clean for me. While she was in school, my doctor arranged for nurses to come in twice a day to change the bandage and other things. My arm hurt so much that I told myself I would never go through this again. The pain where the doctor transferred the muscle from back to my arm was an awesome thing. My back didn't bother me and I thought that was going to hurt badly, but I had to endure the pain knowing I will get better. I had a cast on from my elbow to my hand. I would put ice on it and heat to get some relief; I also would lay a pillow under it, anything to get some comfort. Many times I didn't want to eat. All I wanted was pain pills so I could sleep. When my six weeks were up, I had to go back to Gainesville to get the cast off and the stitches removed from my arm and back. It seemed like it was over hundred stitches in my arm & back. I was tripping because I knew this was going to be painful. I was fine when the cast was removed, but for the stitches I told them to wait. Finally, I let the doctors remove the stitches. It wasn't as bad as I thought it would be. But it was so many I felt they would never finish. I had to start therapy on my arm immediately when I went back to Tallahassee.

I met nice therapists, and they were easy on me at first, but gradually some of the exercises I had to do on my hand were hard. I was determined to do them. I had a little progress, but not that much because of a visit I had with my insurance company. When I went back to my doctor in Gainesville, he felt I should be moving my arm by then; I was somewhat disappointed, but I will never give up on this, no matter what it takes. I will accomplish my goal that I have strived so hard to make a success. I know that, being a child of GOD, His time is not like our time, but you have to keep the faith that one day it will happen. I know the trials and tribulation I went through in my life helped me to get closer with the LORD. I would not make it if He were not in my life. The things I had to go through made me a stronger person. I would get knocked down so many times, but I would get back up. I remember a lady who would pray with me once told me, "If you can't suffer with JESUS How can you reign with Him?" With my walk on this journey and with Christian people in church all the time proclaiming to be child of GOD, how I have been mistreated, talked about, lied on, and treated badly? I knew that I was a GOD-chosen one, and I was picked out of a crowd to be an example. It would hurt me so bad how my Christian folk disliked me for no reason at all. But my spirit let me know there is a difference in being a Christian and being a born again Christian. I can see people say that you are born Christians. How can you say you love GOD and treat your fellow man wrong? I have gone to church sometimes when tears would form in my eyes, and I wanted to break down and cry, but I would look up to GOD and ask Him to help me. He would dry my tears as I felt his spirit moving within me it just like a peace that comes over you. Everybody there in the church I attended was not like that. There were some people who were very nice to me, mostly the older ones.

You know I've always had gifts from GOD; it was hard to fool me. I could pretty much look at a person and I would know what type of person they were. I had associates that called themselves my friends, and GOD would give me a vision of them going back talking about me. There have been so many lies told on me and confusion in the church that it bothered me. Because I am a praying person, GOD delivers me from worrying about what people have done to me. I know GOD's word says revenge is His, so I leaned on GOD, knowing that one day the truth will come out. That's one thing I do not do, play GOD, and I do not like to see people pretending before man and putting on a show to be seen. There was one particular incident when I was in a prayer service, and one lady asked me why I got up and testified...My response was that I have to be moved by the spirit. Whenever I hear GOD's voice, I react, but I do not like to get ahead of GOD. You see when you go through some difficult times in your life, and you know it was only GOD who brought you out, and you are on another level with GOD, I have to be real in everything I do for GOD, because it is not about me but it is about what God do through me to touch the lives of others. He is real to me, I had to hold on and be strong to the Promises of GOD. When I think about what GOD has done for me I get emotional and it didn't matter how I was treated by anyone, because GOD gave His angels charge over me all of my life. Sometimes you have to walk alone, and those so-called friends get out of your way because they hindered and do not mean you any good. I live and I learn. Sometimes it was hard, but that was the price I had to pay in order to grow in the LORD. You have to go through trials. It strengthens you and makes you the person GOD wants you to be.

What I am going to tell next was a big test for me, because everyone cannot handle certain situations, and I know He will prepare you for whatever you are getting ready to go through. I did not understand at the time GOD was speaking to me, but I heard, "Count it joy," over and over. I kept hearing "Count it joy," over and over. My prayer partner, Myra and I would pray very often with each other. You see, GOD has a way of putting you with someone else who will help you at a time such as this.

He will move other people out of your way who do not mean you any good, but you have to pray and ask Him and be sincere. He will answer your prayer; it might not be the answering you want all the time, but He knows what right for you. Whom He chastises, that He loves. My son's girlfriend Rhonda from up north wanted to come to Florida to go to school.

A Wolf in Sheep's Clothing

My son's girlfriend, Rhonda White North, wanted to come to Florida to go to school. She was having problems with her mother, and they were in a big fight. I wasn't sure that I wanted her to come. My prayer partner, Myra Jordan and I prayed about it, and she told me that she felt that Rhonda was trouble. Also, I had the same feeling, but being the person I am, I told her "yes". Although a part of me didn't want her to come, the reason I did it was because she had a son named Jonathon White. He was supposed to be my son's

child, and I wanted to see for myself. I still felt strange deep within. My friend, Vicky Hurse, who had been in my life through thick and thin, no matter what, was there for me. She came along when I picked Rhonda and Jonathon up from the airport. I didn't feel right with the baby. When I saw him, I held him and I felled in love with the baby Jonathon. Still, I knew that Jonathon wasn't my son's child. So, I continued to be nice to them as usual and trying to provide for them also like they were part of the family. When Rhonda moved in, I told her that I am a very clean person and would she keep my house in the same order as it is. The baby was having respiratory problems and I wondered why she wasn't taking proper care of him. Jonathon would cry for long periods of time, which kept us up every night. So I took a day off from work to take Jonathon to the pediatrician. After going to the doctor, he explained to her how many treatments he prescribed for him a day, but she didn't follow through. I started wondering about it, but I kept my cool. I continued to pray with my prayer partner, Myra; we prayed just about every day. The spirit of GOD came upon us, and we began to see many things through Him. When you are close to GOD, he will reveal answers through fasting and praying, and I did a lot of it. One thing I didn't understand about the big picture was, *why would Rhonda want to come here to Tallahassee, when she was in Atlanta, Georgia*...Something just didn't seem right. I felt like he was running from something or someone, but what?

As the days passed, I caught her in lies, and yet I still took care of her. I kept getting off from work to help her find a job and get in school and even medical help. There were times I took the entire day to go around and help her find an affordable car. I have argued with her on several occasions about published the baby down; she wouldn't feed Jonathon, properly. She would give the child to strangers. When I would come home from work, I would prepare hot meals for Jonathon, and that's when hell broke lose. It would upset me to see her give her child to people she had just met and ask them to take care of him while she was away. I would lecture to her night and day, and I even got in touch with her mom, who stayed up north. Rhonda was very angry with me. One afternoon my spirit led me to stay home and Rhonda questioned why I was still there. What she didn't know is that my spirit or intuition has never failed me yet. Time passed, and within ten minutes, the doorbell rang. It was a tall man for Rhonda, She goes out with the baby, her sleeping attire still on, and the baby wasn't dressed properly for the weather. She stayed outside for hours, and I was furious. I called her mother once more, but it didn't do any good at all. It was like one thing after another happening.

 I introduced her to a friend of mine, because I knew he would talk to her and would try to help her out with her baby, and he did just that. I felt they were sneaking behind my back, and she pushed the baby off on him, especially on the weekends, as much as she could. I would get unknown numbers on my caller id at different times of the night. I had specifically told Rhonda not to give my phone out. She would lie and say she didn't, but I did have this happen before. It was an unpublished number.

One night she was screaming, and someone was coming in the window, and the screen and window was up. I had sleepless nights from then on. I was at the end of my rope. There were times when she would leave and go out with Jonathon and the apartment manager, whom she had met. I would question her about giving Jonathon the proper dosage of medicine for his sickness. Eventually, I influenced Rhonda to attend church with me; I felt that maybe even a few bible study classes here and there and prayer meetings that she attended would help her. Rhonda joined the church during a revival, and she was baptized.

One night Jonathon was sick. My nephew, John, came over and took Rhonda and Jonathon to the emergency room. I was going, but I had my daughter, who was 10 years old with me, and she was fast asleep. The baby was so sick the doctor gave him shots of medicine in the mouth. I had called constantly, because it was so prolonged. He was still having breathing problems. She started repeating things over and over again, like leaving Jonathon with my niece and nephew. They told me she gave the baby something with alcoholic content. I knew I had invited the devil into my home, and I needed to do something to correct the problem. Rhonda would lie about how much money she had, although she could afford to keep her nails, toes and hair done. I constantly prayed and prayed. That is when I started looking for another place to live. She got involved with my friend and his sisters.

One afternoon, I had received a call from Rhonda stating that she was in Atlanta, Georgia. visiting her brother who lived in Atlanta, and that she would return soon. I was fine with it, because I knew that my lease was up soon and I wasn't going to live like this. We had mysterious things happen like break-ins at my home, which had never happened until she had moved in. When Rhonda got back from Atlanta very late one night, she came in with all these bags, saying that her brother had bought her these things for her and her baby. I just went along with her story.

The next day I took Rhonda to TCC to get enrolled for college, and I continued to take her around to look for employment. I had a talk with Rhonda and asked her if Jonathon was my son's child, and she said that she would prove it by having a blood test done. It never happened. One of my friends that was good friends with Paul said that Rhonda mentioned to him that she had no clue who was the baby's father and that she was a stripper back home in Michigan. After all the things she told me about all the fights she was in with groups, it didn't surprise me about Rhonda. I felt like I had to be a mother to her and a grandmother to her child, but I couldn't get that bond with the child, like I have with my granddaughter. Why not with this baby? I questioned myself. He was the cutest baby and my love for him didn't stop. I did all I could, because I knew he was an innocent child who was helpless and my heart always went out to children and elders. I do not mistreat anyone, no matter what nationality they are. I finally told her that she needed to get her own place, because I needed my personal space. I even offered to let her use some of my furniture, and that's when we went looking for a place to stay for her. I would never be comfortable where I was staying. I finally found a nice area, and I moved there. Before we went our separate ways, I thought that I would make peace with her, so I invited her to my mother's house for Thanksgiving. We all went up with my niece and nephew, who were driving my car. My mother and siblings were very nice to Rhonda and Jonathon; they fell in love with Jonathon. One of my sisters had noticed strange things about Rhonda. She couldn't wait to tell my family that Jonathon was Ryan, my son's baby. Gloria came to me and told me that Rhonda was trouble and that she didn't believe Jonathon was my son's baby. I told her I knew and that God had shown me the truth also, Rhonda left the baby with my family. Then, she started flirting with my nephews, but here is a person that would tell me all the time she is in love with my son, Ryan and would cry about him. She even told me she went to a psychic about my son, and I told her my psychic was God and that is whom she needs to put all her trust in. My family started asking questions and seeing more of Rhonda and figuring her out. What really upset me was on the way back, when my brother and cousins were coming to help me move. During the move, I gave her my livingroom furniture, linens, towels, clothes, and some bedroom furniture. I had always had weird feelings about Rhonda and gradually the pieces were finally being put together. My son came home from Atlanta, and my family and I had warned him about Rhonda, although he wouldn't listen to us. Rhonda had tried to turn my son against me, because she knew I had figured her out. Ryan had moved in with Rhonda, and she was working and he stayed home and kept Jonathon. I would leave work on my lunch and go back where I would see him giving Jonathon breathing treatments. She had dressed the baby up with the finest clothes you could buy for a child. My little girl loved Jonathon and she would take him around, stay over there just to be with Jonathon. They would come over and I would fix dinner for them, and occasionally I would keep Jonathon so that they could go to the movies. I got on my son about finding a job, and he would tell me how he could not because he was taking care of the baby. But I knew it was a trap. Sometimes love is blind, and it took him a while to come around. He told me that he was going to leave the baby with her friends and how sick Jonathon was with a fever. I told Ryan that they should have taken Jonathon to the hospital. One day my son called very upset, and told me to meet him at the hospital because the ambulance was taking Jonathon there. He was upset and Jonathon had had a seizure. I left right away, devastated. Because Ryan was crying, I knew it had to be serious. Rhonda and I got there and the doctor said it wasn't good at all, he said Jonathon could die. I began to cry and so did Rhonda. We were all basket cases; the doctor said they would have to operate on Jonathon. We were all in the waiting area, I called a friend to inform Rhonda's mother, which she did. Her mother called crying and asked what had Rhonda done now. She was going to come down, and Rhonda seemed like she was calm but I wasn't and my friend got there and she comforted me. She said all sickness is not about death that he was going to live.

Police officers had approached my son, Ryan and Rhonda questioning them about the situation. We would take turns staying up there, when her mother arrived she stayed with me. We were talking and I was telling her everything, even when her daughter went to Atlanta to see her brother and she responded he never told me that Rhonda came to visit him. She even said that she wouldn't be surprised if Rhonda were shipped back there in a box. My son and one of her male friends almost had a confrontation because of the rumors they were telling Rhonda's mother. I knew what type of child I had, and how he helped me with his sister Raven, by combing her hair and making sure she's neat. I knew he wouldn't have harmed Jonathon. It looked like every time I came to the hospital you would see her strange friends. Then her mother started acting strange towards my son and me. They were plotting something against my son. She moved out and was staying at the hospital. She even went and told Human Resource Services that we didn't want her there with the baby. I told her that I thought I was a grandmother, too. Why was it just her? My son came home crying, trying to say that I hurt him. He began to tell me how Rhonda dropped Jonathon one night, and I asked why he didn't tell the police. Why was he protecting her? All I could do was pray that Jonathon would survive. I spoke with Rhonda's mother; they were going to meet with her daughter and my son the next day, but she told me they said I couldn't come. I was convinced that I knew something was going to happen on Tuesday morning. My son dropped me off at the salon where I had a hair appointment and he went down to HRS. I kept calling the house because I knew he should have come and picked me up from the salon by now. I began to worry, I knew something wasn't right. I had my hair stylist to drop me off at home. I was pacing back and forth and everything was coming together. Did he get into a car accident? Or what? I got a phone call from Ryan's friend saying Ryan was arrested and the station parked my car.

I started screaming, his friend said that he will bring my car to me and I thought I was losing it. I called my family and my friend, Myra, who was my prayer partner. My mother tried to talk to me and let me know they were here for me. They had to call around for an attorney. I cried and I cried and I cried; something spoke to me and said "Get up. And go to bible study…" I did, and when I got back from bible study I didn't want to look at television. I was so afraid, I didn't want to go on living, I didn't want to see anyone not even go to work, because I didn't want to face anyone. I knew how some people are when another is down. I knew I had God and my family on my side, and my prayer partner, but in my state of mind, I wasn't sure about anything else. I stayed home from work for almost two weeks, but my supervisor was so understanding, he told me to take all the time I needed. My friends came to my rescue. One supervisor even came up to me and said I was highly respected, and that made me feel good. I knew I had to go through this for the level God wanted to place me on and I had to pay a price to strengthen myself, to do what God had placed in me that I wasn't doing. Also, it was a lesson for my son, God was trying to get his attention, and he had gone astray. He admitted everything I said happened, even a wake-up call, but he was rebellious to God. I would visit him in jail, because his bond was fifty thousand dollars. We wanted the right lawyer. I would witness to other young men that were in jail, also, and I would pray with my son while he was there. It would hurt me to see him there, but I felt he needed time to seek the Lord.

I still was trying to support my son while he was there, but I had to tell his sister, Raven, although her father didn't want her to know what was going on so he kept her away. I had to fuss at him constantly, I didn't trust him, because they all were with her and her friends I didn't want him in my home. I told him to drop my little girl off and leave when I told her my girl wouldn't stop crying she keep saying my brother didn't hurt him, it was Rhonda who kept hurting the baby. I didn't realize that it was going to affect her that much, but it did. She was withdrawn and saying she hated Rhonda. She also said Rhonda's mother and her dad, Aunties and friend was talking about Ryan. When I approached Raven's father, he said he didn't have anything to do with it. I knew he had some involvement with Rhonda. One day justice will be served and God knows, and he will fight my battles and I know he is in my corner. I kept praying with my friends and trusting God, because I knew my son was innocent and also knew I am a God's child, and that they didn't want to mess with me. But it was hard. Though I needed to put this in God hands, during this time the baby was getting better and HRS took the baby out of the system and given him back to his mother. All my family came to town for their support on the day of court. Rhonda was trying to complain at the same time giggling, because they would not lower the bond. My family paid five thousand dollars to the lawyer and five thousand dollars to the bail bond. But, I said ok that her laughing would turn into crying one day. She will reap what she sows. My son got out on bail and Rhonda and Jonathon went back to Michigan. There are still some unresolved issues left behind. Everything is not over yet with my son. But I am trusting in my God to fix it. My family and I paid close to fourteen thousand for this case was treated unfairly. During the upcoming trials we was informed that all the money that was spent, the attorney did not do his part and I got tires of the family coming up with the money, that's when a public offender took the case. Even though the attorney didn't do right by my child the first go around when he did it to me and my child, he did it to God. He will give account of everything he has done and that's with anybody.

I thank God for Myra and my family and other friends that helped me get through this ordeal. I was very discouraged in the members of my church; only a few had supported me and that really hurt me. Instead, many wanted to talk about my child and don't really know what took place. I know it was blown out of portion, but the truth will stand. I've never thought I would experience cold hearted religious people like the ones that pretend to be so spiritual. One thing about this, many of them couldn't go through the trials I have been through and still come out on top. I learned that just because you are in church, the devil's having his people there also. With the many things I was accused of and also my son, many will see my face again, and they will have to answer to God. Because God has placed me there for a reason. I didn't want to go back, but I had to be obedient to God. I have learned that you are not going to be liked by everyone, anyway, especially when you belong to God.

I have experienced God's anointing; my gifts have been blessed and I have experienced the power of God. I will have my second book, because I still have so much to cover this chapter is to be continued. I can say be careful, boys and girls, men and women. Who you choose in your life could cost you your life. Let God choose your mates; it will keep you from a lot of pain and heartaches. May God bless you as you read this book. I pray that it will be inspiring to you spiritually.

As I leave, I give you words of advice. Take your problems to Jesus and leave them there. He will solve them in his own time. Weeping may endure for the night, but joy will come in the morning. Jesus loves you and He cares. His ways and thoughts are like no other. He is the superior and He has lives in his hands. Having polio and not using but one hand didn't stop me; some things I had to learn to cope with. I learned not to let a problem or handicap get the best of me; learned to use strategy and take an inventory of myself of how, why, and what I can do to improve my life. I had to stop having self-pity and stop putting my self down. I would repeat this to myself. I can do all things through Christ who strengthens me. If I had not placed God in my life, I do not know where I would be, even with the state of mind at times I was going through. I have always been a praying person, even when I was a little child. I prayed, even though I didn't understand the fullness of the effects of prayer, changing the lives of others, which is so powerful. For that, somewhere you can set aside time to be quiet and meditate on God to feel His presence and enjoy spiritual growth. There were times that I've found myself periodically asking how I wanted to get closer with God. If we all live and learn to depend on and trust God, stop putting man before God, and really pray for our churches, children, and nation, this world would not be in the condition it is in now. We all desire to excel, but we do not want to go through trials. No one comes to God except through faith, hope and loss. I feel good about myself, and I know that I am a child of God, that life is not a bed of roses, you have to take the bitter with the sweet. Love has the power to heal every aspect of your experience, as long you don't give up on God. If we continue with real persistence in any endeavor, we will be rewarded for our effort. Sometimes it takes moving some of those friends that are attached to you, or family, or anything that can be a block in your path, especially telling all of your business to people. That is a no-no; get wise, see the light, everybody is not happy for your success or getting ahead. I lived and I learned the less people know about your business, the better you can succeed in life. I realize how true this is, based on my own life. Misery loves company. Ask God for guidance, wisdom, discernment, and understanding. Success comes from a process of continuing our ventures very persistently, with faith, not doubting God, and just knowing that and believing. Hold onto your dreams, don't let go, no matter how it seems, for faith knows far beyond the things you and I can see. If you stand on it, faith always wins. Through our faith, we shape our lives. I could have given up many times, but deep down I knew I was going to succeed in life, that my God is rich, and He has the key to my life. Sometimes we are exercising our power of faith, but not always in positive ways. I myself don't like to be around negative people because it dampens my spirit. Our life experiences are actually the source of our faith; we place our faith based on our experiences in life. Our life experience has an impact on our point of view and our attitude. So if you are always speaking negative things or positive things, you are speaking things into existence. What you speak is what you get, but faith in God is most importantly a choice of direction. When life's challenges are getting us down, and we feel our pain and our depression, we need to discover new and deeper levels of our power of faith. In truth, the more in touch we get with our God, the more space we create for our faith to grow. The more faith we feel, the more powerful we become. It occurs to me that true faith, faith in God knows that life doesn't always feel like a smooth and fascinating ride guided by someone in whom we have unconditional faith. Our life has bumps, sometimes bruises. We may sometimes fear being thrown from the carriage. At times, it seems we gain too much speed and we go out of control or we get totally stuck and the wheels won't turn. We may imagine there is no one steering, and no one knows or cares where we are headed. However, in fact, our journey is being guided all along. It is our faith that brings us this knowledge, and as we choose the direction of our faith and stay close to the faith that softens our hearts, we experience an ongoing revelation of God's eternal love. It is encouraging us to love everybody, not take life for granted, Life is too short. Take advantage of it and make the best of it, even little things. For instance, when I had my surgery I wanted a shower all the time, but you have to do without it because of the schedule at extended-care two or three days a week. You don't realize how good life is to you until you get down. Where as you have depended on others. It's the little things that can make you a stronger person. Now, whenever there is a challenge, I see it for what it really is. I learned to give thanks to God always. As I progress on my spiritual journey, I discover that our earthly experience is not the real issue. It is our spiritual life that is at stake. First seek the kingdom of God, and all these things will be given as well. Would you rather gain the world and lose your soul? Everyone has that decision to make. My soul and being with my father in his kingdom, that is more important to me. The deepest desire is the desire to experience unity with God. God love is omnipotent, omniscient, omnipresent, all power, all knowledge. Take God at His word. He said before His word shall fail, that heaven and earth will pass away. That deep every problems, you have is in the bible, anything you want to know, but you have to read. When you do that and get understanding, don't read just to be reading. Pray for wisdom and knowledge of His word. I love God and my advice is always having a relationship with God. I know what He is to me and always will be to me in my life, without Him, I am nothing, but, with Him I am somebody greater than him that is in me. Prayer helps us establish our right relation with God. Prayer has power in the face of odds that seem to be impossible and overwhelming. I thank God not only for the spiritual healing, but the opportunity to experience the depth of negativity without that experience. I learned to have compassion for others, and through my warfare with the devil, how to resist him with the powerful words of God; I never would have awakened to God's word, the spiritual keys to our happiness and fulfillment here on earth. May God bless you. I hope my advice will inspire many of you and make a change in your lives. Try Jesus; you will never go wrong. Although our experiences in life are different, everyone has gifts that open doors to opportunities, available to us from God. Always remember that with God guiding our way, we can overcome any limitation that our upbringing or anything from the past may seem to impose on us. We put behind us whatever it is that has tended to limit us, whether it is family and friends who have said we were not capable of doing things. We know with God all things are possible and as we listen to the divine wisdom and follow the guidance, we will receive all things possible for us.

Be Positive...

Be positive...Fight the good fight of faith
Don't give Satan an inch...for God commandments
You need to obey;

Failures are the work of the devil trying to destroy
your soul.
Stop being negative and be positive in
Reaching your Goal;

Do your best in everything you strive to be
For Jesus died on the cross for you and me;
God didn't give us the spirit of fear
Though his grace and mercy is always near;

Problems are the guide for you to get to the next level.
But you must go through it,
If you want to go to heaven;

Even when struggles come our way
And we sow our faith a seed
Remember Jesus is on the main line;
He will supply your every need;

So dedicate your life to Him this day
Be positive; be positive Jesus is on the way...

Surgery

On January 28, 2000, I had surgery on my left foot. My entire left foot was changed dramatically, a screw was now inside of my big toe, and the other toes had pins in them. After waking up from the surgery, I was experiencing sharp and throbbing pain, which had brought me to tears. I stayed in the hospital for seven days, and then I was transferred to an extended-care facility. The day of my arrival, I met an occupational therapist named Ivy, who introduced herself to me and was very kind and concerned about my well-being. I was very impressed with how the staff I knew from the past and the new staff all made me feel welcome. Sometimes, we don't understand the reasons for different circumstances. This surgery was very different from the other surgeries in the past (and believe me there were a lot of surgeries). I thought I would be in the hospital and maybe go to extended care for a week and get out, but it didn't happen that way. I said LORD, I know you have me in here for a reason, and at the time I didn't know what it was. Shortly I found out that I had to witness to various ones that were going through illness and battles.

You never know what other people are going through, until you have walked in their shoes or that you touch them by your testimony. GOD spoke to me, so I can be an inspiration for the lives of people here in extended care. You can make a difference in people's lives. I know I have angels here that have truly touched my life. I was filled up with tears and I know GOD gave me favor with Him and with people. The social worker, Irma Daleen, was one of my angels. I had a doctor appointment at the Tallahassee Orthodepedic on February 14, and my cousin was going to come along and support me, but her work schedule was changed and I didn't know who was going to take me. Gratefully, Mrs. Irma went with me and was very supportive when I was getting my stitches removed. The tears ran down, as I was experiencing tremendous pain. She is a very classy and sophiscated woman who has the warmest and most caring glow about herself, A person that loves people and who is a very important in my life.

Roommate at extended care

During my stay at extended care, I had a roommate around my age, named Jane. She was very quiet and very friendly, although she was very ill. She was a diabetic patient, and she told me she had a severe heart attack. She stayed in the hospital a long time, but was transferred to extended care for a short time. Because of her illness, she had to go back to the hospital. I met her parents and boyfriend; they all were very nice to me. I would pray for her and my heart went out to her and her family, because of her sickness; every time I looked around, she was getting blood taken. We didn't talk as much because she would sleep most of the time, and she would tell me she was so tired. At times, she wouldn't even go to her therapy because of being weak and tired. Of course, I was gone the majority of the time in the morning, because of my physical and occupational therapies. I didn't know her except for a short period of time. On February 13, 2000, Jane was so happy. I had a flashback of that night. Her boyfriend gave her presents for Valentine's Day. He gave Jane a gigantic card and flowers and stuffed animals expressing his love for her. That afternoon she stayed out of the room for a long time. I never experienced it ever during my history in the hospital. When Jane finally came back into her room, she told me she had diarrhea and it must be something she ate. She told me that her boyfriend had asked her to marry him and she accepted. She didn't know what to do because her mother didn't care for him much. During that time, she had me calling her parents for her to see if they were coming up, so they wouldn't both come at the same time. I would give her my advice about her boyfriend from my spiritual view. I could see how much he did love her; everyday he would come and be by her side throughout her sickness. I told her to do what made her happy. This girl looked like she weighed about ninety pounds, if that much. That night, the nurses were in and out all night; I might have gotten two hours of sleep. Jane was up and down to the bathroom. I couldn't do anything but pray for her; I was afraid that she was dying that night. When morning came, they isolated her and moved me to another room. I asked different nurses how Jane was doing. that Thursday, she was placed back in Tallahassee Memorial Hospital instead of extended care. I still continued to ask about her. On February 19, 2000, a Saturday afternoon, one of the nurses came into my room and told me that Jane had passed away that morning. My heart went out to her family. I heard her mother telling her she wish she had another girl just like her. I really felt so bad for her boyfriend that I was looking for their phone numbers to express my sympathy but wasn't successful in finding them. So much sadness filled my heart and that day I could picture her face; her fingers on her hand were rotting off, but she didn't want the doctors to amputate her hand. My really major concern was her soul and if they were saved. It's not about death, because we all have to leave in this world, but I have peace in my heart that the ring she received from her boyfriend before she died gave her peace.

Tillie Hogans

My Life

My life was blessed from my mother's womb;
I knew I had a story to tell soon;
At the age of two I was paralyzed from my head to toe;
When the Doctor said there was no hope;
Although that's when God stepped in and said this is my child
I have the last say so;

I always knew that I was a child of God;
Even when my problems seemed so hard;
I couldn't solve, there were times in my life I was at the end of my rope;
But the love of Jesus was there and I knew it was hope;

He took me in the cradle of his arms;
With his love and compassion;
I knew I wasn't going to be harmed;
I do not dwell back on the past of the memory lane;
For I am not the same
My life has changed when I was down and I couldn't see on my own;
God's love and God's word were the only things that made me strong;
When I was down to the last dime
He step in and He was right on time;
My life, He holds my future in His hands

God's Miracles in My Life

Even when I am in sin;
Jesus forgave me over and over again;

I want to thank you God for my life;
You never left me; instead you are always on my side.

Tillie Hogans

My Journals

Week *One*:
Week one I was in lots of pain, I didn't want anything to eat the majority of the time, but I would drink plenty of fluids. My first week in the hospital, I did meet some incredible people especially males that kept me laughing. I was in Tallahassee Memorial Hospital for seven days. Some of my co-workers and choir members from church came out to visit me. They brought me things I like to eat, flowers, and money, but my appetite still wasn't there. My deacon, Al Dennis, that I think so much of, really was concerned about my well-being. He came to see me also and always has been there for me.

It made me feel special because of all who came out to support me. I really would like to thank *Sherika Frazier* who was drawn to me, she was an ex-co-worker of mine, but she is always helping me with my book to help my dreams come through and is a big inspiration in my life. I had therapy seven days a week, and I like to be there around 9 a.m., because I enjoyed the therapists and their exercising that they showed me.

Ivy Murillo - Occupational therapy—called Beamer, but I called her Red Hair. We had become very close. She helped me a great deal. She focused on activities of Daily living—bathing or cleansing, dressing, and exercising.

Gaylon Willis - Occupational therapist—over-achiever. He helped me with exercise to strengthen my arm.

Beverly Simmons - Occupational therapist—assisted and taught me to transfer to the bathroom facilities and also provided stimulation with my arm.

Sylvia Phillips - Occupational therapist—always liked to pat me on the top of my head. She would help me on the weekend with different activities.

Rhonda Craig - Physical therapist assistant who had a big heart. She assisted me in different exercises such as kick-out, which would keep my legs strong. She also trained me how to transfer from wheelchair to vehicle.

Spencer Moore - Teddy Bear—My first weekend he helped with the upper-body exercises with other exercises on my arm.

Eusibius Jinks - Physical therapy assistant—would help me on the lower part of my body. When Rhonda wasn't there to help me in and out of my wheelchair he filled in.

Sue Smith - Physical therapy assistant—would help me on the lower part of my body. She was very humorous and had a good spirit.

Irma Daleen - Social worker—my guardian angel. she went with me to my doctor's appointment. She was very concerned about my well-being. She has a big heart.

Week *Two*:
I was transferred to extended care, where there were faces and names I remembered from the last time I had visited five years ago. Everyone was so nice, during that week.

I had two roommates. The first one was an elderly lady; I stayed there about three days until I was moved into a semi-private room. I stayed there for almost a week before I got someone in my room. I had requested a private room yet there were none available. I started my therapy the following day. I was so impressed how people got so attached to me; it seemed like the whole staff were drawn to me.

I would sometimes like to go out to the lobby to write things for my book. Dietary was getting on me about my meals and said if I didn't like my tray order, I could request something that I really wanted, although I would barely eat.

Earthly Gallon - Spiritual guardian—she would give me some words of encouragement.

Bart Baxley - Bartman (Recreational Therapist) informed me on all the recreational activities for the month. He was a good listener. He also went with me to place another cast on my foot.

Wendy Roots - Activity Director—my ticket was drawn the first night I won a Valentine's stuffed bear.

Rosa Green - Physical therapist was very serious about her patients exercising.

Ebonique Carney - FAMU student who volunteered—she would comb my hair and help me perform some of my exercises. She would take me outside for walks and transport me to different areas.

Maria Parolinoy - A nurse who would give me my medicines although she would go overboard doing what she could, for which I was very grateful.

Sheree Porter - Speech therapist—was very nice to me. It helped me recover.

Week *three*:

I was still the person who always had a smile on my face, but I was ready to go home. I still had all my therapists laughing, and they would tease me about not letting me go home. I pretty much had my way, when it came to a shower I always had my way of talking someone into giving me one. I wanted one in the morning and one at night, but, sometimes it didn't happen that way. I was always witnessing to people; they would come around me with different problems. I encouraged them if they were out of church to go back. Sometimes though, I had problems, but after hearing others' problems, mine were small. I would wake up during the night praying for people's requests. Sometimes I would cry because my heart went out to them. That was the week my roommate died. I could tell that she wasn't going to make it, She was so sick, but I was glad I was there for her when she needed me. It was very short, but I did help her out. The third week, more young teens were coming there because of car accidents. It was so sad to see a young guy cry when they were having him do some therapy.

Week *four*:

This was a very exciting week for me; I had learned that I would leave the following week. I felt that I had done my mission for God while I was there and it was time for me to depart. I was very impressed about the impact I had on people during my stay. I still continued to write my book and kept in touch with friends. I love people, and I like to do whatever I can to bring smiles to their faces. I did my transfer from wheelchair to car. It was one of the last phases I had to accomplish with the occupational therapist. It helped me to master everyday routines, and I went to my therapist daily. After my departure, I had to visit my therapist once a month. I began to eat a little more, and my therapist was amazed. My spirit was overwhelmed because I knew my journey would be better. You are going to have all types of obstacles in your way. They are placed in your life to make you a stronger individual. I knew what I had to do when I left extended care and I had to be able to walk once they removed my cast, no matter how painful it may have been.

I knew I was going to be challenged and it made me very assertive, but you have to want and have the faith to overcome any obstacles in your way. On March 1, 2000, I said my goodbyes to everyone. I felt a peace inside because I knew God was smiling on me. I knew he empowered me with love and words to say to people while I was there.

His purpose for me was fulfilled. My first day home wasn't a good experience. I tried to maneuver in the wheelchair with one hand. Although I didn't let anything stop me and I am the one who likes to show the devil you will not defeat me no matter what. I knew God ordered my steps. I had to be patient but I knew day by day I was headed for success. I had an occupational therapist come in to help me with my exercise and my daily baths. They both were limited until the cast came off and the pins were taken out. I was counting down for March 13, 2000 to come. I am the one who always like to have something to do and it bothers me if I can't get it done. Even so, I took some risky chances while I had the pins and cast on. I would fuss at my son if he left any dishes in the sink. It would make me so furious, and I would stand up on one foot and clean my dishes and put them up. Also I would mop and dust my home in the wheelchair. There were times my first week that I went to church to give thanks for what God has been to me in my life. I almost fell, but because I always was determined and God has always been there for me, I knew it was only his grace and mercy that had brought me through. On March 13, 2000 one of my friends picked me up to go and remove my cast and pins. I was so afraid, but I was the happiest person in Tallahassee. That's how I felt after arriving at orthopedics. I had x-rays on my foot first. Since my x-rays were good, the doctor told my friend that she could come in, because he knew that I was afraid and remembered how I was when the stitches came out. My eyes were huge when I saw the instruments he had in his hands to pull out the pins. I asked them to give me something but I ended up getting numb in cold water at first. I looked away. I could feel the pressure from pulling. When I turned around, I was devastated to see how long those pins were, but I was amazed that the pain wasn't bad at all, that I didn't feel anything besides the pressure. It was painful to stand up, but I felt a load was lifted off me once the cast was removed. I was on my way, starting to make steps.

I know that the very ground on which I stand at any time is sacred, for wherever I am, God's presence is with me. I know all the things I have gone through from a baby until now were challenges to me. My ministry is by my life to stand as a witness to the greater life of faith, reaching out to embrace those who are going through and feel that they do not have a way out. Let nothing trouble you; let nothing frighten you. Wherever God is, you lack nothing. God alone is enough. There is time where you need to be alone with God. Even though I was getting help from therapists to walk, and I was very determined to make the most efforts, that's where faith comes in. I would get alone with God and pray and ask Him to help me, because I was ready to do His will, whatever He guides me to do. I would hold on to the bed and slowly walk around. No matter how hard the pains were, I wasn't going to let pains get the best of me. God knew my heart and He knew I was real; that's one thing about God, no one can't fool Him. That night I went to bed, I saw a vision of me walking the very next morning when the therapist came. He said, "Ok, I need you to begin walking with the cane." At first, fear came over me. I would be afraid to make that first step. I began to repeat to myself that I could do all things in Him that strengthens me. Satan moved out of my way when I said that, and I began to walk from my bedroom to the living room.

Conclusion

In conclusion, you cannot run away from your problems. You cannot distance yourself in order to look back and assess your situation. There are times that you have to face your problems head-on and ask God to order your steps in whatever you are going through. If you want to know how blessed you are, think back to a situation you thought was right for you, and further down the road you found out how wrong you were. Do your best in life. Do what you can in striving for what you want to be. Remember you are still growing. You are learning; you can be negative if you allow yourself to go through dark circumstances. We think negative thoughts and come to the conclusion that negative is all we expect. We are limited as to what we can see. We see and expect very little for ourselves because the world or darkness has little to offer. No matter what you are going through, remember God loves you. God is our power, the source of our strengths and our good. We are faced with difficulties, and have given up on God. God will use the opportunity to demonstrate how powerful He is. God does not give up on us, He gives us chances and other chances all over again. God will fight the battles when we move out of His way. The greatest, the ultimate questions, are about God and my relationship with Him. Nothing in life is more important than this. Nobody told me that the road would be easy and it's not; having polio and the fears in facing the world wasn't easy. It was often confusing and frightening to make a shift away from the familiar in order to embrace the unknown. Yet it was necessary labor that I had to undertake in order to grow. No matter how difficult, challenging, or hard it may seem, changing is necessary when the time comes to free ourselves from the confinement of mental, social, emotional, or physical boxes. When it came to that point in my life, I had to go on. The longer I fight against it, the harder and more painful the fear becomes. When I make up my mind to change gears, everything connected changes too.

I can say opportunities are always there for you and me. God always has a door open for us. You can miss many blessings because of your attitude instead of getting up and getting on that train on time and not standing there letting blessing continue to pass you by. I remember the saying "if you let the devil ride, the next time he will want to drive." You see, I am speaking from experience that the devil will play all kinds of tricks on you. He will have you thinking things that are not there. He will play on your intelligence; he is an enemy. The devil will get you out in a situation and leave you out there to hang. Keep your eyes on GOD, lean not on your understanding. Put your trust in him. Every day is not going to be sunny; there will be days that you are going to have rain in your life. Believe me, it only enables you to hold onto God's unchanging hands. He will pick you up every time you fall. This will determine if you really love God like you said you do. Are you willing to stand when you feel there's no hope? Each storm will make you that much stronger. I have had my share and probably some one else's share of ups and downs, but I didn't give up, even when I wanted to. I still stood, whether you know it or not. God lets some of His people go through harder trials than others. The reason for this is that some people are not equipped to cope with spiritual, mental, and physical things. God knows we can stand, even though I was the one in the family to be afflicted with polio. I felt that my other sisters and brothers wouldn't be able to handle it. I thank God for wanting me to be that one to go through and to pick me out of the crowd and let my testimony be a blessing to the world. I am always a witness to people and have many people come to me telling me there is something different about me. I want my light to shine so people can see chariots in me. Letting the world know in the midst of my fear, the weakness of my strength. Jesus was always there. In the midst of confusion, He has given me peace, when my trials and burdens overwhelmed me. He breathes on me and sees me through. I thank God for the good as well as the bad. It is good to give thanks to God. No matter what is going on in your life today, remember, its only preparation you can think, you can feel. Thank God you are alive. The key is knowing the powers of God are in your corner and on your side, and that we are fully equipped, perfectly capable of facing any situation, under any circumstances and coming out on the top. I'm writing this book to help you understand that tomorrow might be like today. The evening might not be like this morning. The next hour might not be like this hour. This is not the time to put off doing what you know to be right. This is not the time to procrastinate. This is not the time for contemplating. This is not the time to be luke warm. I am writing to increase your confidence in God and His word. God will see you through any challenging experience. God will see you through everything in life. God's presence will sustain you. God's love will strengthen you. God will see you through darkness to light, uncertainty to confidence, sorrow and fear to faith. Remember that the bible teaches that faith is the only approach to God. For he that cometh to God must believe that he rewards them that diligently seek Him. The bible also teaches that faith pleases God more than anything else. Without faith it is impossible to please Him. I know where I've come from, and I know why I'm here. I know where I'm going, and I have peace in my heart. I would always tell some of my co-workers that I do not limit God, and I don't put a price on God. Then face that there is no limit to God; there is no limit to His wisdom. There is no limit to His power. There is no limit to His love or mercy. So stop putting a limit on God. Sometimes a change of perspective may be all that it will take to transform a painful, frustrating, or shameful experience into an empowering growth experience. I had to stop looking down and start looking up to God. Whether you believe it or not, your thoughts and words determine your reality.

When you change your mind, you can change your life. In the midst of my difficult and challenged experience, I was growing, which made me give myself time to examine, question, and explore the principles at work and my emotions. I had to fall, and I knew it was God that picked me up, but I know you have to go through it to appreciate God, yourself, and what life has to offer. You see, God becomes personalized in you, through you, and as you. God becomes an individual, loving presence that knows your needs and guides you in the right path. Once I have done my best, I can I wait on answers or a voice to tell me what to do, and I stand on God's words. I know deep down that having made the connection as each present moment comes into being, there will be action for me to take and successive steps will lead to an outcome that is best for me. I know nothing will stop me; I would always say a quitter will never win, but a winner will never quit. That's my motto. No matter how hard my battles were, I would still get up and step out on faith. The following next day, I wouldn't use the cane the therapist gave me to use. He said, "I am going to discharge you." I was doing great. He also said he didn't think I would walk so soon. But I know who holds the future in His hands and that's God. I recommend Him to you who are reading this book, if you don't have Him in your lives. From that day on, I was improving more and more from surgery. I wanted to go back to work on March 27, 2000. My doctor said it was up to me, I asked God to order my steps; my God did. Everyone at work was so nice to me and concerned for me not to overdo it and to complete half days. I would always say to myself I could do all things through Christ that strengthens me. There comes a time in your life when you have to press your way. Always put your trust in God. He was always there for me with a plan for my life. God simply asked that I trust in His divine guidance. I will go where all the things that God has done for me through his love and his word lead. I like to close by recommending the practice of meditating and praying and centering yourself on the indwelling of Christ and staying focused on Him. I promise you it will make a difference in your life. Let go; let God. Doing that will help you surrender your troubles, your dreams, your needs, and most of all, your life to God. Who will guide you to happiness and success and serenity? When the devil makes any situations or problems look bad for you, remember that God will turn everything and make it good for you. May God bless you and I wish you all success on this journey and may your soul's salvation will be in good standing with God.

God works through His perfect will. Keep your head up high, because through my ups and downs, I learned the battles were not mine but God's. He will see you through. I hope as you read this book you will discover, or perhaps rediscover, your special place, your special time with God. You will realize that there is nothing impossible with God. Put your trust in God and pray, because a man should always pray and faint not. I pray that you will experience such a realization of God, of God's presence, and of God's help, that you will know that God is real in your life. Just invite Him in, and I can assure you God will do the rest. Your life will change for the better. Be steadfast and immovable, but stay anchored in the Lord.

There are so many *positive things* that have influenced my life and others.

I pray that this book will inspire positive things to happen in your life. When your friends let you down, think positive, as if maybe they weren't your true friends in the first place. When things just aren't going your way, think positive, maybe God has other plans in store for me.

In addition, if it had not been *Reverence for GOD*, I would have died at an early age. HE had a mission on earth for me from an *early age*. GOD has always been right there to protect me. Mastering my *handicap* was a difficult task in my way. I acknowledged my disability and learned how to deal with it. It's important to realize that you have to love yourself first before you can love others. We all have a handicap, whether it's physical, mental, or spiritual; we just have to learn how to cope with it in our daily lives. You have control over what *steps* to take in your life.

Just remember to have faith in the divine and to treasure every moment spent here in this life. For the roads are getting tough to follow and the paths are very dim, but look to the hills of heaven for your strength. Special thanks for my mother, sisters and brothers, my son and daughter, Vicky Hurse, Myra Jordan, Gloria Richardson, Sherika Frazier and John Higgins who was there for me and played a very important roles in my life.

Tillie Hogans

The Crippler

The crippler is known to others as paralytic poliomyelitis, a virus known to distort human bodies. Poliovirus enters a vulnerable host in contaminated drinking water or through contact with a contaminated surface, such as unwashed hands. After passing through the stomach, the virus reaches the intestine, where it establishes itself in the cells of the intestinal lining (the "gut mucosa"). There, it replicates in infected cells. In most cases, this results in a fleeting, uncontrolled diarrhea, or it may be completely asymptomatic. Unfortunately, the virus is not always so malignant.

In approximately 1% of infections, the virus flows from the intestine into the bloodstream and nervous system, until it reaches the motor neurons and causes death. The exact device of the virus's flow through the body is still not known. Some theories have been proposed. Some clusters of cells located in the intestine, better known as Peyer's Patches, seem to supports the beginning stages of the infection. Even though the Peyer's Patches are strongly linked with the body's immune system, it was assumed that the parasite migrates from there into the bloodstream. Once in the blood, it gains access to the nervous system, where the breakdown of motor neurons (those which control muscle movement) results in paralysis.

A few researchers have discovered that the parasite may be related directly through nerves, rather than blood. In a genetically designed mouse, the virus migrates to the spinal cord and then a form of replication is formed, the first limb paralyzed is the one which was injected. It may be the case that the nerves still connecting the injected limb to the body are damaged before injection, the virus is not able to spread to the spinal cord, even though blood still flows between the limb and the body. This implies that the virus travels through the nerves to reach the spinal cord.

Poliovirus is spread by the "fecal-oral" route, which, in spite of its unpleasant name, is a familiar path of microbial infection. The virus can still be remote from human feces and sewage. In places where the raw sewage enters a watershed without treatment, polio can originate in rivers, lakes, and streams. When a vulnerable person drinks water from one of these, the virus enters his or her digestive tract.

In extremely contaminated conditions, nearly most offspring are open to the virus throughout infancy, when the bug with polio is most discovered,. These offspring attain ultimate protection from the virus. Once big offspring or grown offspring are contaminated, they are subject to be paralyzed or killed by the bug. While humanity improves its cleanliness those are possible to be out in the open to polio soon after in life, if at all, so the parasite starts to crop up in erratic cases. Those who are more fortunate are the first to benefit from enhanced cleanlines; they are frequently the primary populations to experience these epidemics.

This primary requisite is followed by conformational changes in the virus's capsid which are believed to arrange it for uncoating. The receptor is in use by the cell with the approach of endocytosis, which is almost inevitably involved in PVR's normal purpose. The disease has started to gain a protein on the cellular plane in sequence to gain access and launch an infection. This is a familiar approach of various creature and plant viruses.

The poliovirus receptor is expressed in several human being tissue types, in fact with some tissues, such as kidney, which are not standard sites of mass poliovirus replication. Why doesn't polio duplicate in these cells, if its receptor is obtainable to allow it in? There are two theories:

Either the virus's replication is barren in these cells at certain step after access. The disposition of a virus to duplicate only in specific tissue types is called "tissue tropism," and is a working section of research for researchers studying many types of bugs. Polio infects cells in the lining of the intestine and can transfer to nerve tissue, where it causes the feature pathology of paralytic poliomyelitis. In the other model, the virus element must be full into the cell by a procedure called receptor-mediated endocytosis, a method regularly used by cells to take in food and signal proteins. Based on this method, the disease then reveals inside a partition that forms in the cell, and the genome is revealed into the cytoplasm. There is minimal experimental data to support either method, so both are taken into consideration on related possibilities.

The whole poliovirus RNA particle is formed into a separate long "polyprotein." This huge particle then attaches itself into subsections and eventually into the single particles which are involved in replication and packaging. Several of the viral proteins also cause the breakdown of the cell's messenger RNAs while still allowing the viral RNA to be changed, causing the cell to be more competent virus factory.

To its positions in distributing up the polyprotein, one of the few proteases is composed of breaking down most of its cell's own protein synthesis.

The protease does this by cleaving a component of the cell's version mechanism which is important for regular protein production, but which the viral RNA does not find essential. Breaking down the host's RNA version serves a double function for the bugs: first, it frees up more ribosomes to interpret the viral genomes, and second, it insures that the cell will die and break down, revealing the progeny virus particles after they have been assembled.

RNA viruses have a special problems when it comes to duplication, as the cell does not have the required methods to replicate an RNA molecule (the cell duplicates DNA, which is transcribed to produce RNA, and RNA is defined to produce proteins). In other words, the virus must have its own RNA

God's Miracles in My Life

duplication substances or have a method for producing them once inside the cell. For polio, the replication functions are carried out by a viral, RNA-directed RNA polymerase. In other words, it reads an RNA form and produces a new RNA molecule of the opposite polarity. Because RNA is single-stranded, the first round of duplication produces a single antisense, or complementary, molecule, analogous to a printing plate where all of the letters are the opposite. This antisense form is then used to create a positive-sense duplicate of the original genome. As these new genomes grow, they can also act as more messages for the cell's translation methods, forcing to higher levels of viral protein production.

Karl Landsteiner stated that a virus rather than a bacteria caused polio in 1908. Polio has almost certainly caused paralysis and death for most of human history.

The oldest understandable identifiable check to paralytic poliomyelitis is an Egyptian stele (stone engraving), which is over 3,000 years old. Cases of poliomyelitis were supposed to be rare in ancient times, though, as sanitation was usually inexpensive. With better methods in waste disposal and the spread use of indoor plumbing in the 20th century, epidemics of polio began to happen routinely in the process stage, mainly in cities during the summer. Because sewage was thrown away from the drinking water supply (a process which helps fight a number of other viruses, including cholera), offspring were much less likely to be infected with polio and gain protective immunity. As the children got older and began playing with others, swimming in public pools, and going to school, they were more likely to be exposed to the virus, which was then more likely to cause paralytic poliomyelitis.

Thus, while the Salk and Sabin vaccines have significantly reduced the threat of paralysis by polio, there are still good reasons to study this virus.

By the time of the Great Depression, paralytic poliomyelitis was perhaps the most feared disease known. Polio struck fast, there was no cure, and it crippled its victims for life. Hobbling on crutches, rolling in wheelchairs, or lying immobile in giant iron lungs, the legions of sufferers accumulated from year to year. Even the exact mechanism of polio's transmission was a hotly debated subject for many years, so many areas were placed under strict quarantine when cases of the disease began to manifest themselves. Only the fear surrounding AIDS can rival the feelings people had about polio in the first half of this century.

President Franklin Roosevelt declared a war on polio during his administration, and the tremendous resources of postwar America were brought to bear on the problem of developing a vaccine.

In the early 1960s, the work bore fruit, first with the Salk vaccine, and soon after with the Sabin virus strains.

Salk used chemical and heat treatment to kill poliovirus, then injected this inactivated virus into patients. The proteins of the destroyed virus "taught" the patients' immune systems to recognize polio, and they were then protected from subsequent infection. Sabin's approach was to grow the virus in the laboratory under a variety of conditions, allowing it to accumulate mutations. Ultimately, this resulted in an attenuated virus, which could be given to a patient orally. The weaker virus replicates normally in the intestine, but cannot grow well enough to invade the central nervous system. Once again, the immune system "learns" to recognize polio, and this confers protection.

As part of the "War on Polio," researchers Albert Sabin and Jonas Salk, taking different approaches, developed effective vaccines against the virus, and a widespread immunization campaign rapidly brought it under control in developed countries. The Salk vaccine is an injection of chemically killed virus, which "teaches" the immune system to recognize the virus and eliminate it. This vaccine confers lasting, but not always life-long, immunity. Sabin's vaccine is given orally, and contains attenuated, live viruses of each of the three polio serotypes. The attenuated virus replicates in the patient's intestinal tract and induces immunity, but is not virulent enough to cause paralysis (except in rare cases).

Once the Sabin and Salk vaccines were proven effective, the disease was rapidly eradicated throughout most of the industrialized world. The economic effect has been enormous; it has been calculated that the polio vaccine pays for the costs of its development approximately every three weeks. The benefit to the United States alone for this single breakthrough runs into the trillions of dollars. The social impact has been incalculable. The crutches, wheelchairs, and iron lungs of polio victims have at last been banished from children's and parents' nightmares, at least in the developed world. the CDC has recently changed the protocol for childhood vaccinations to use a combination of the two vaccines.

In other parts of the world, where money for health care is scarce, the Sabin vaccine is preferred, and it is this vaccine, which has made the eradication of polio a realistic goal. WHO officials called on member nations to step up vaccination and avoid complacency as the campaign enters the final months of what many experts regard as its most crucial phase—the global elimination of paralytic polio cases.

Even if the eradication effort misses its first deadline, it has already produced impressive results: from 1988 to 1998, the number of cases of poliomyelitis worldwide dropped from 35,000 to 5,673, or 85 percent. The last case of the disease in the Western hemisphere was found in Peru in 1991, and the last case in the WHO's Western Pacific region was found in Cambodia in 1997. Reservoirs of the disease remain in Africa and Southeast Asia, and outbreaks have also occurred in Eastern Europe since the collapse of the Soviet Union. Though some observers have suggested that the campaign may take until 2003 to eliminate paralytic polio, the WHO delegates asserted that the year 2000 was still a reasonable goal.

The nations of the world are listed here according to the progress they are making towards eradicating polio by the year 2000.

The first step is a high level of routine immunization. National immunization days can then push the virus to the edge of extinction.

Thereafter, every single case of child paralysis must be investigated and if proved to be polio - surrounded by another immunization blitz.

Polio virus cannot survive for more than a few months without a human host.

By the year 2000, all doors should be locked against the virus.

About The Author

My name is Tillie L. Hogans and I am 50 years old…Born on March 16, 1953 in a small town named DeFuniak Springs, Florida. As the third oldest child, I was born to William and Ruth Hogans and grew up with four sisters, two brothers and one cousin.

I was stricken with polio at the age of two and have lived with this handicap for all my life.

My father was killed in a car accident when I was at a young age and my mother, with the help of my grandparents, raised eight children.

As a single mother, I raised one son, who is now 23 years old and I am still raising one daughter, who is 14 years old.

Because of the struggles that I have overcome in life, I am dedicating this book to GOD, My Mother, Ruth Hogans; son, Ryan Hogans; daughter, Raven Whitehead and to everyone that have inspired me over the years…

Printed in the United States
1342300001B/134